A
History of the
Christmas Crib

A
History of the
Christmas Crib

The Word was made flesh
and dwelt amongst us

Tim Everson

© Tim Everson, 2023

Published by Tim Everson

A CIP catalogue record for this book is available from the British Library.

ISBN 978-1-7390846-0-8

Book layout and cover design by Clare Brayshaw

Prepared and printed by:

York Publishing Services Ltd
64 Hallfield Road
Layerthorpe
York YO31 7ZQ

Tel: 01904 431213

Website: www.yps-publishing.co.uk

Contents

Introduction

I have always loved Christmas cribs. As a child we had three or more cribs so that there was one in each room at Christmas: the original Woolworth's crib, the inherited crib, the French crib given by my sister-in-law, the crib we made from a *Woman's Weekly* magazine guide, and others. My mother was very fond of dolls houses which she made and changed constantly and it was the same with cribs. The figures would generally remain the same but the buildings they inhabited would be spruced up or demolished at regular intervals. When my mother died in 2011, I inherited the cribs and I had already bought a new crib for my family when I married in 1994. In the last twenty-five years I (and others) have added to the crib collection and many of these are illustrated in this volume. At some point I began to wonder about the origins of the Christmas crib. I remembered from my school days that it was supposed to have been invented by St Francis of Assisi in Greccio in Italy in 1223 but it has since been found out that this is not quite the case. St Francis created a life-size 'stable' in the cave church with a real ox and ass; no statues were involved. He was, however, certainly the inspiration for the cribs that followed.

What is a Christmas crib? For the purposes of this book, a crib is a three-dimensional representation of the birth of Christ, usually but not always with moveable figures. Strictly speaking, the crib is the manger where Our Lord lay, and later came to mean the building wherein the figures stand, but there are many 'cribs' which simply consist of the figures themselves. These figures are Baby Jesus with his parents Mary and Joseph at the very least, usually accompanied by an ox and ass, shepherds and sheep, Three Wise Men and perhaps an angel. In America, they call the Christmas crib a crèche (derived from Greccio), and 'crib' means something else again, a bedroom or den!

The birth of Christ in Bethlehem has been depicted in art since Roman times, but generally in a two-dimensional context. The Nativity also came to be represented in the church by tableaux or mini-dramas in the liturgy, which later developed into mystery or miracle plays. This book aims to trace how these two sources (and St Francis) led to three-dimensional cribs and why, and how they have remained a staple of Christmas decorations and devotions ever since.

Acknowledgements

My thanks to the parishioners of the Sacred Heart Church, Wimbledon, especially those members of the Friendship Group and the Newman Society who encouraged me in this work. Also, many thanks to Georgette Vale for our talks about cribs and crafting, and for permission to use pictures of some of her beautiful cribs. Finally, and especially, many thanks to my wife, Shaan, for her support of this project and her many insights and historical knowledge which have made it a much better book.

CHAPTER ONE

The Birth of Jesus, the original mangers, and the date of Christmas

The Christmas crib is a way of visualising or reconstructing the story of Christ's birth and, for Christians, it can be used as an aid to prayer. The birth of Christ is what the great Christmas celebration is all about; when God sent his Son to save us by having him born as a human baby to the Virgin Mary (also known as Our Lady). Early artistic representations of the Nativity, and later Christmas cribs portray different elements of the Christmas story drawn from a number of different early literary sources.

The Birth of Jesus in the Bible

The birth of Jesus is mentioned in two of the Gospels of the New Testament, Matthew and Luke. They were both written between AD 70 and 80, after the destruction of the Temple at Jerusalem by the Romans, and were intended to make sure the story of Christ would not be lost whilst some of his apostles were still alive to speak about him. There are some intriguing differences between the Gospels as different people remembered different things or wished to place the emphasis on what was important for them at the birth of Jesus and its relationship to different people and events.

In Matthew, Mary is betrothed to Joseph but is found to be pregnant before they marry. The Angel of the Lord appears to Joseph in a dream and explains that she is pregnant by the Holy Spirit. Joseph marries Mary and she gives birth to Jesus. He is born at Bethlehem in the reign of King Herod the Great (who died in 4 BC).

Some wise men come to Jerusalem following a star and looking for the infant King of the Jews. King Herod asks his chief priests where the Christ, the Messiah of God, was to be born and they tell him that it was at Bethlehem in Judaea, according to the prophet Micah. Herod sends the wise men on to Bethlehem but asks them to let him know when they find the Messiah so that he too can worship him. The wise men follow the star to Bethlehem and enter the house where the child is with his mother Mary, and worship him. They give gifts of gold, frankincense and myrrh. They are warned in a dream not to return to Herod and go home by a different route.

The Angel of the Lord appears to Joseph in a dream and warns him to flee to Egypt because Herod wants to kill the child. When Herod realises that the wise men are not coming back to him, he has all the children aged two and under killed, in Bethlehem and the surrounding district. (This is known as the Massacre of the Innocents.) After Herod dies, the Angel of the Lord again appears to Joseph in a dream to say that he can return. Herod Archelaus, a son of Herod the Great is now ruler in Judaea, so Joseph decides to take his family to Nazareth in Galilee instead.

Much of what is apparent in certain representations of the Nativity or in modern day cribs is present here, but where is the Angel Gabriel, the innkeeper and the stable, the shepherds? Let us see what Luke has to say.

Luke gives us a far more detailed version of events which includes the story of the birth of John the Baptist, some three months before Jesus. John the Baptist was the son of Elizabeth, Mary's cousin, and would help prepare the way for Jesus' mission in later life. In Luke's gospel, the Angel Gabriel visits Mary at Nazareth, where she lives, and tells her she will give birth through the power of the Holy Spirit. He also tells her of her cousin Elizabeth's pregnancy. Mary visits Elizabeth in her home town in the hills of Judah (traditionally Ein Kerem near Jerusalem), and Elizabeth recognises the greatness of the child Mary is carrying. Mary stays with her until Elizabeth has her baby.

We then get the decree of Caesar Augustus about carrying out a census of the population, which means that Joseph and Mary have to travel to Bethlehem. There, Mary gives birth, wraps the baby in swaddling clothes and lays him in a manger because there is no room at the inn. The Angel of the Lord appears to shepherds in the fields nearby to tell them that their saviour, the Christ, has been born, and a host of angels appears praising God. The shepherds hurry and find Mary and Joseph and the baby and tell everyone what the angel had said. Eight days later the Holy Family travels to Jerusalem for Jesus' circumcision. So, a fuller account, but no mention of the wise men here, the star, or King Herod and the Massacre of the Innocents. Also, while Matthew mentions a house, here we have the manger but no real notion of where that manger is.

There is a further source from a later period: the apocryphal Gospel of James, written in about AD 150 and known to the early church fathers, which combines elements of both Matthew and Luke but adds further details which the author thought were important. The apocryphal Gospel of James (purporting to be written by an elder half-brother of Jesus, son of Joseph from a first marriage) begins with the story of Mary. It names her parents as Joachim and Anna and describes her birth and upbringing, where she becomes a holy virgin at the Temple in Jerusalem.

She marries Joseph at the age of twelve, when he is an old widower with two sons, but remains a holy virgin, sewing the curtain in the temple which screened off the Holy of Holies. The Angel Gabriel appears to her when she is sixteen and tells her she will have a baby by the Holy Spirit. She then visits her cousin Elizabeth. When she returns, obviously pregnant, Joseph is very distressed as he thought she was still a virgin dedicated to the temple. The Angel of the Lord appears to him in a dream and explains. Mary's obvious pregnancy cannot be concealed and she is hauled up before the priests to explain herself, as is Joseph. They are eventually believed when they swear they have not had sex and complete an ordeal in the desert.

The census of Caesar Augustus is then mentioned and Joseph puts Mary on a donkey in order to travel to Bethlehem. On the way the time comes for her to give birth, so Joseph finds a cave for her and goes to find a Hebrew midwife in Bethlehem. Joseph meets one on the way and introduces her to Mary as his betrothed, but not his wife, because she is a holy virgin. Time suddenly stands still as the Saviour of the World is born. A bright cloud appears in the cave. The midwife is amazed and praises God. The light fades and there is the infant Jesus who suckles Mary's breast. The midwife leaves the cave and meets a woman called Salome and tells her of this virgin birth. Salome says: "As the Lord my God lives, if I do not insert my finger and examine her condition, I will not believe that the virgin has given birth". (This is very reminiscent of doubting Thomas wishing to put his fingers into the wounds of the resurrected Christ.) The midwife tells Mary to brace herself and Salome inserts her finger whereupon her hand begins to burn and wither. She kneels and begs for forgiveness. The Angel of the Lord appears and tells her to touch the child. She does so and is miraculously cured. A voice then tells Salome to say nothing of this until the child enters Jerusalem.

This apocryphal Gospel then follows Matthew closely in introducing the wise men coming in search of the Messiah and being interrogated by Herod. They leave Herod and enter the cave where the star stands over the entrance. They offer gifts of gold, frankincense and myrrh. They go home by a different route and King Herod decides to kill all the children under the age of two. In fear, Mary wraps the child in swaddling clothes and places him in a cattle manger. Elizabeth and her baby, John the Baptist, hide in a cave which miraculously appears, but her husband Zacharias is killed by Herod's agents.

This Apocryphal Gospel of James often struggles for coherence and is uncertain in its geography and casual in its chronology, reasons why it was not accepted into the canon of the New Testament in the 4th century. It was well known, however, in medieval times and is the origin of the story that the manger was in a cave and that Mary travelled to Bethlehem on a donkey, both eminently sensible notions. The midwife and Salome, sometimes known as the two midwives, appear in many depictions of the Nativity in the early Middle Ages, but have mostly fallen out of favour before the development of the crib. St Jerome spoke out against the idea of Mary having a midwife. He said Our Lady would not have needed one because Jesus would have given her a painless and straightforward childbirth. An easy comment for a man to make perhaps! It is indeed far more likely that Joseph would have sought out a midwife to help Mary with her first birth, especially in a strange town when they were unable to find a room at the inn.

We have mentioned the donkey Mary rode, which is generally taken to be the ass of the ox and the ass shown in Nativity scenes as early as the 4th century, but where does the ox come from? Our final source is not a gospel but the Book of Isaiah from the Old Testament, dating to the 8th century BC. The book of Isaiah contains many prophecies which refer to Jesus, and when early Christians read it they discovered in Chapter 1, Verse 3: 'The ox knows its owner and the ass its master's crib'. This was seen as a clear reference to Jesus' birth, and so later Christians assumed an ox and an ass must have been present. In the 13th century, Blessed James of Voragine (c.1230–1298) added the opinion that, while the donkey was there because Mary would have had to ride one, the ox was brought by Joseph to sell so that he could pay the census tax. More prosaically, where there is a manger, there are surely cattle to be fed and the apocryphal Gospel of James, whilst not mentioning an ox, does say that the manger was a cattle manger. As a late source for the ass, Mary is always depicted as riding a donkey on the Flight into Egypt in various works of art.

The Cave at Bethlehem

Since Jesus was born at Bethlehem, this became one of the places for Christians to visit. We know that people venerated at a cave there, believed to be his birthplace, as early as the reign of the Emperor Hadrian (117–138), because Origen (185–254) tells us so. Hadrian covered the Christian shrine with a temple to Adonis, a fact noted by St Jerome. This temple lasted until 326 when it was pulled down by the first Christian emperor, Constantine the Great. His mother, St Helena, built a new Basilica of the Nativity on the site, incorporating the cave. St Jerome visited the Holy Land in 385 and saw the cave and the manger within. He imagined how the scene must have looked 400 years previously but was disappointed to see that the original cradle made of clay had disappeared, presumably destroyed by Hadrian and the Adonis worshippers. In its place was a silver cradle, probably donated by Constantine among many splendid gifts he gave to the sanctuary.

Jerome lived in a nearby cave and was buried there in 420. His greatest achievement was the translation of the Bible from the original Hebrew and Greek into Latin, known as the Vulgate Bible. His followers St Paula and St Eustochium, also lived nearby and founded a convent. Together, all three taught Latin and Greek in a free school, and ran a hospice for travellers and pilgrims to the holy cave. Visitor numbers fell in the 5th century due to various riots and incursions, but in the 6th century the Emperor Justinian greatly enlarged the Basilica of the Nativity and incorporated into it Jerome's cave and tomb as well as the Nativity grotto.

Unfortunately, in 614 the Persians under Khosrow II invaded the Holy Land and destroyed many Christian sites. It is rumoured that the Basilica of the Nativity survived only because a frieze featuring the Three Kings was thought to represent Persians. Although the Emperor Heraclius regained these territorial losses soon afterwards, the Roman Christian recovery was short lived. By 640, the Muslims had swept through the Holy Land, making it more difficult for Christians to continue to worship at the place where Jesus was born. When the Crusaders conquered the Holy Land in the years following 1099, they further decorated the Basilica with paintings of saints on the pillars, and made the front door much smaller (The Door of Humility) to stop people riding their horses into the church!

Fig 1: The Church of the Nativity, Bethlehem with the Door of Humility to the left

After the victories of the First Crusade, the sanctuary came under the control of the Roman Catholic (Latin) Church, whereas previously the Orthodox Church under the Byzantine Empire had been in charge. (The churches had formally split in 1054.) The Byzantine Empire was the surviving Roman Empire with its capital at Constantinople (Istanbul), after the western Roman empire had been conquered by various Germanic tribes in the 5th century AD. Saladin drove the Crusaders out in the late 12th century, and the Orthodox Christians regained control. Today, the Greek Orthodox Church owns the nave and the Nativity Grotto where

Christ was born, the Armenian Orthodox own a chapel to the right of the altar, whilst the Roman Catholic Church have a new church of St Anne's on the left side and own the cave of St Jerome adjoining the Nativity Grotto. The cave of St Jerome gives a better idea of what the caves looked like in Jesus' time since the Nativity Grotto is now floored with marble and hung with lamps.

Fig 2: The Grotto of the Nativity

Under the altar is set a large silver star with a central hole, so that worshippers may touch the actual cave floor where Jesus was born. There is also a nearby altar dedicated to the Magi, the Three Wise Men from the East. At Christmas, an icon of Mary and Jesus is placed in the Grotto, but there is no crib or figure of Baby Jesus here, since the Orthodox Church does not have statues of any sort.

The Manger in Rome

Even before the arrival of the Muslims, Bethlehem had never been an easy place to reach for Christians living further away in the western Roman Empire and so, in the 440s, Pope Sixtus III erected a chapel at the church of Santa Maria Maggiore in Rome which contained a replica manger. This was the first church named in honour of Mary as Mother

Fig 3: The Grotto of the Nativity. The site of Jesus' birth

of God (Theotokos), a title she had recently been given at the Council of Ephesus in 431. Christians could pray there whilst imagining the birth of Jesus, and it seems that this church was also the site of the first Christmas midnight mass.

In the 7th century the chapel received five small boards made of sycamore, reputedly from Jesus' manger, and brought to Rome to save them from either the Persians or the Muslims. Since St Jerome assumed, perhaps on good authority, that the original manger had been made of clay and had been destroyed, these boards have a doubtful reputation, though it seems likely enough that they came from Bethlehem and were connected with the Basilica of the Nativity in some way. Since their arrival, the chapel has been known as Santa Maria ad Praesepe, St Mary at the Stable. (Italian cribs are known as 'Praesepes', stables, and the existence of these pieces of wood may be the reason the Nativity is often depicted in a wooden stable rather than a cave.)

This chapel in this church became the focus of celebrations of the Nativity as the power and prestige of the Roman Church grew in comparison to the Eastern churches. A portrait of Our Lady, supposedly drawn by St Luke, is also kept in this chapel and brought out at Christmas. Whether the pieces of board are part of a manger or not, the idea is the same; trying to picture the scene as God sent his son to earth in human form. If an actual piece of the crib is there, or a silver replica, as at Bethlehem, it is an object that helps you to concentrate and focus. So, as we see, the first 'cribs' were the real or supposed mangers of Christ himself from Bethlehem.

In the 13th century, when the Holy Land was overrun by Saladin, the retreating Crusaders removed the body of St Jerome and placed it in the chapel of St Mary at the Stable in Santa Maria Maggiore church in Rome. At about the same time,

Fig 4: The Reliquary of the crib in Santa Maria Maggiore in Rome

Arnolfo di Cambio sculpted the first known Nativity scene consisting of free-standing figures, although it is clear from earlier Christian authors, such as Jerome himself, that worshippers often imagined the Holy Family standing around the manger with them. Other churches in Rome also set up chapels with replica mangers and the cult of Christmas began to grow.

The Date of Christmas

People could contemplate the birth of Christ at any time, at these manger chapels or elsewhere, but when did December 25th become fixed in the church's calendar for this great Christian celebration of the Nativity? Pope St Telesphorus (c.126– c.138) is rumoured to have created a Nativity feast which was moveable, like Easter, and could occur anytime between May and December, but the evidence for this is slight, as is the idea that he held the first midnight mass at Christmas. The Feast of the Epiphany, when the Magi visited and God was 'made manifest' (Greek: Epiphanes) for all the world, is actually an earlier celebration than Christmas, which only became fixed in the 4th century.

In the 3rd century, the Romans were very keen on the worship of a personification of the sun, Sol Invictus (Unconquered Sun), who appears on coins as late as those of Constantine before he became a Christian. A great feast to Sol was the winter solstice in December. Christians saw

Jesus as the light coming into the world at the Nativity when God was made flesh (became incarnate). In about 330, December 25th was settled on as the date to celebrate the birth of Christ. This was the date which, from the time of the Emperor Aurelian in 275. had been the feast day of Sol Invictus, the day when the sun was at its weakest and fires needed to be lit to encourage its rebirth. It was an obvious date to use as the birth of Christ to try and encourage pagans to turn away from the sun god and worship the true God made man.

The celebration gradually extended in the Western Church into the twelve days of Christmas, beginning with the birth and ending with the Epiphany. In 529, the Emperor Justinian declared Christmas Day a public holiday. This sacred festival and the four weeks of Advent as preparation for Christmas, were confirmed at the Council of Tours in 567. From the 5th century the season of advent began to mark the beginning of the church's year, as it still does. The Eastern Orthodox Church continues to use January 6th (Epiphany) as its Christmas Day.

As for the actual year of Christ's birth, Dionysius Exiguus, a monk working on the calculation for Easter dates in the 6th century, devised the BC/AD calendar. Most scholars agree that he put the birth of Christ on 25th December, 1 BC in his new system, though some suggest AD 1 (there is no year 0). This system of dating became popular in the later 8th century and is now used almost universally. However, Dionysius was uncertain of the exact date of the birth of Christ because the Gospels do not specify it exactly enough. We know now that Herod the Great, who looms large in the Nativity story, actually died in 4 BC in the BC/AD system, so it is accepted that rather than AD 1, Jesus must actually have been born in about 5 or 4 BC, when Herod the Great was still alive.

CHAPTER TWO

Before St Francis

Church Liturgy and Drama

Drama, in the form of the church liturgy and, later, mystery plays, had a great impact on the development of the crib. To have a crib in a church presupposes knowledge of the Nativity story, and the story develops from the Gospels and Apocrypha through the order of service in the church at Christmas. Early writings on the Nativity bring out the mystery of God the creator come to earth as a little human child. The babe in the manger is also our omnipotent God. How can you describe that? How can you imagine that? St Ephraem (c.306–373) wrote a hymn on the mystical birth of Christ, the source of all creation. Shepherds come to worship the God who created both them and their sheep. Ephraem also brings in all the labourers in the fields and the vintners come to worship 'the new vine'. Christ was sometimes described as 'the new vine'. Carpenters come to worship the prince of artisans who told Noah how to build the ark and Moses how to build the tabernacle. Newlyweds come to worship the child of Mary, the bride of the Spirit of God. Children come to see the child who (as God) gave them games to play, and women and young girls come and give thanks that God chose a poor woman to be his instrument. It is from St Ephraem that the idea came to place everyone in the crib, not just the shepherds and kings, because God came for all of us.

In the early church, homilies telling the story of Jesus often took the form of dialogues, with a deacon taking the part of an uncertain Christian or a non-believer asking questions and having them answered by the priest. This was done in order to explain Christianity more easily to interested visitors. These homilies also began to incorporate actions:

tableaux or simple drama, perhaps to help attract people away from the classical drama and circus games that were still popular in Roman towns.

The church authorities were not always happy with this. Bishop Tertullian in Bologna in the 5th century was opposed to any sort of drama in a church service, but there were more moderate bishops elsewhere who could see the attraction. There were always some restrictions, however. Popular songs and instruments were banned, as were certain gestures and poses copied from classical theatre. The Council of Laodicea in AD 363–364 decreed that only members of the clergy could stand in the pulpit and declaim or sing.

Nevertheless, Christian drama slowly developed in association with Christmas. A sermon of St John Chrysostom (c.347–407) states that: 'I hear the shepherds playing on their pipes, no vain song, for they are singing a celestial hymn while the Seraphim sing their doxology and all are keeping the festival of God seen on earth.' Does this mean that people were playing pipes and singing as an accompaniment? Possibly. Things seem a little more explicit in St Romanus' canticle, written in the 4th century. Here, Mary hears the Magi approaching and goes to open the door for them and explains St Joseph's part in the Incarnation to them. St Joseph and the shepherds sing, and then the Magi explain their origins in Persia, Babylonia and Chaldea and how the star drew them to Bethlehem. They also speak of Herod and their gifts. The canticle draws to a close with Mary playing the lead part as both Mother of God and Mother of mankind, pleading for them and invoking the blessings of her son. The Encomium of St Proclus (died c.447) has a similar series of scenes and the earlier works of St Ephraem mentioned above were very popular throughout the Greek speaking East Roman (later Byzantine) Empire.

By the 6th century, as related by Sophronius (560–638), dances as well as music were being included in Christmas homilies and these lasted for quite some time, especially in the Eastern Church. The format of these Nativity dramas was fairly settled by the 6th century and followed a series of set scenes, no doubt with some variation. The first scene featured the prophets and relevant passages from the Old Testament. Then came a dialogue between God and the Angel Gabriel where the angel is told not to frighten the Virgin. (In the Orthodox Church there is a tradition that the angel first appeared to Mary when she was fetching water from a well and *did* frighten her! She ran away, and Angel Gabriel had to try again at her home.) The next scene in the play was the Annunciation, with Gabriel and Mary, followed by a scene with Gabriel and Joseph. The Voice of God reassures Joseph and then there is a scene of the Council of Devils, who argue and plot against what is about to happen, which ends part one.

The second part begins with the journey to Bethlehem and is followed by the Nativity in the Grotto, the fetching of the midwives, the hymn of the angels, the adoration of the shepherds and the adoration of the Magi, and concludes with a scene of the Fury of the Devils. Then the Magi visit Herod, who consults his advisors, and later the Massacre of the Innocents takes place, Joseph has a warning vision and he and Mary escape on the Flight into Egypt. The cycle ends with a fight between Christ and the devils. The scenes with the devils, although unusual to our eyes today, are there to show the never-ending battle between good and evil, with the Nativity as the point in history when God sent his Son to help us in this fight. (Some Neapolitan cribs in the 18th century and later would place a small devil under the manger as a reminder of these scenes.)

There was surely a manger present in these scenes but it is also quite probable that the church altar functioned as the manger. Today at Christmas, Catholic churches often place the statue of Baby Jesus on or before the altar during the Christmas Eve service, after which he is placed in the crib. In the 8th century, Patriarch Germanus wrote that the altar was both the manger and the sepulchre of Christ, and Pope Hadrian I (*r.*772–795) also stated that the 'altar is the manger'. The Byzantine Empire still had a foothold in south Italy and Sicily in the 8th century and these dramatic Nativity services were also seen in the Western Church but in a much more sober form. Indeed, when Liutprand, Bishop of Cremona, visited Santa Sofia in Constantinople in the 10th century he was scandalised, claiming that the church had been turned into a common theatre. Little did he realise that the Roman Catholic Church, shortly to be separated from the Orthodox Church following the great schism of 1054, was in fact moving in the same direction.

The earliest drama in the Western Church was concerned with Christ's passion and crucifixion, but a drama concerning the Nativity soon followed. It was performed before or after matins on Christmas Day, or sometimes as an introduction to midnight mass. For the earliest drama, a veiled portrait of Our Lady with Baby Jesus was placed on the altar with a light above for the star. Two groups of deacons stood either side of the altar representing the midwives and the shepherds. The midwives sing: 'Whom seek ye in the manger?', to which the shepherds reply: 'We seek Christ our Lord, a child wrapped in swaddling clothes according to the angel's word.' Other pieces could be added, such as readings from the Old Testament, and the finale was the midwives pulling away the veil to reveal the portrait. This simple drama spread through Italy to France, Germany, Spain and England, no doubt with local variations.

There are repeated mentions of the portrait being placed in a manger, but no description of what the manger was like. In 1160, Gerhoh of Reichersberg mentions a 'crying Child in the manger with His Mother', suggesting human actors playing the part. The shepherds' part in the drama grew, and they later wore shepherds' clothes rather than their deacons' robes. A boy was placed up in the roof of the church to be an angel guiding them to the crib while a choir of 'angels' sang. After their conversation with the midwives, they remained in the choir and sang further hymns and responses. At the end of the service, the priest turned to them with: 'What have you seen, oh shepherds say? Tell us what appeared to you on earth?' They reply: 'We saw God our Saviour born, and round Him the choirs of angels, alleluia, alleluia!'

For the Epiphany there was the *Ordo Stellae;* a play which grew in elaboration from the 8th to the 12th century. The manger was also the centre of attention here and the shepherds played a role, showing the Magi the way to go. By the 11th century, the number of Magi has been fixed at three, representing the three gifts of gold, frankincense and myrrh, and also the three continents, Europe, Africa and Asia. The Magi also have names. Melchior is old with a grey beard. He is supposed to wear a violet tunic and cloak. Gaspar (or Caspar) is young and fair, beardless with a red cloak. Balthasar has dark skin and hair and wears a red tunic. All these clothes were to be cut on the 'Syrian pattern'. The *Ordo Stellae* calls the Magi 'kings', which is the way these three personages are generally referred to and depicted from about this time. This idea that the Magi could be called kings comes from Isaiah 60:3,6, seen as a prophecy about Christ's birth. Isaiah says: 'And the Gentiles shall come to thy light, and kings to the brightness of thy rising. The multitude of camels shall cover thee... they shall bring gold and incense'. Psalm 72, verse 11 was also seen as referring to the Three Wise Men at the Nativity: 'Yea, all kings shall fall down before him: all nations shall serve him'.

The *Ordo Stellae* even has some stage directions. These tell us that the kings must walk seriously as they follow the star, which is a lamp pulled by a string hanging from the roof. The kings might carry their own gifts or have attendants to carry them. One of the king's attendants should have his face blackened and Balthasar should talk gibberish to show how foreign he is. The kings visit Herod and then arrive at Bethlehem, indicated by another light over the altar. They prostrate themselves before Jesus and proffer their gifts whilst singing of their gifts' properties: gold for the great King, incense for the true God, myrrh for the suffering and death of his humanity. There would then be scenes of their dream (in which they are warned not to return to Herod) and of their departure. These could be acted in different parts of the church, for the people to follow around. Churches then had no pews or seats so this was easier to do than it would be today.

The meeting between the kings and Herod was probably one of the favourite episodes, and Herod became the villain of the piece. When it was his turn to appear, he would come in with his attendants, all bearing wooden spears. Herod would throw down his spear in a temper and then read one of the lessons. Meanwhile his attendants would rush about beating the clergy with inflated bladders! The death of Herod was later depicted with as much realism as possible. Further scenes were added to the drama, like the Massacre of the Innocents and the list of the prophets.

The *Carmina Burana* in the Benediktbeuern text from the 12th century has a great many scenes with the original music and, while the dramas were in Latin, verses in the vernacular began to be inserted as well, especially in France. It is probable that the clergy thought that latitude in the performance of these sacred dramas would provide a counter to the bards and jongleurs of the town square, but the rowdiness of Herod and later inserted scenes of the prophets with Balaam and his patient ass, or the Massacre of the Innocents, led to vehement opposition from the stricter clergy, especially Gerhoh of Reichersberg at the end of the 12th century. The Abbess of Hohenberg pointed out that all depended on the spirit in which the dramas were performed and she wished to separate the ancient traditions from the more modern innovations. In 1207, Pope Innocent III denounced the license of the dramas and those who took part in them, although later in the century the Vatican said this was not meant to put a stop to Passion and Nativity plays staged in a spirit of reverence. This is no doubt the reason why St Francis felt he needed to seek permission from Pope Honorius III to set up his crib in Greccio in 1223.

The Nativity in Art Before St Francis

Before we approach St Francis, we should also look at how the Nativity was portrayed in art from the late Roman period. The earliest representations we have are carved onto the sides of late Roman sarcophagi, or painted and carved in the catacombs of Rome. The most interesting thing here is that the scenes sometimes take place in a stable or shed, not a cave or grotto. It seems that artists found it difficult to depict a cave or difficult to place figures realistically in a cave setting and settled on the stable as the place where animals were more usually kept in Western Europe, as opposed to the more common cave shelters of the Middle East. The ox and the ass feature prominently, their breath keeping Baby Jesus warm as he rests, usually bound tightly in swaddling clothes and laid in a manger.

Fig 5: Roman gravestone from Naxos showing the ox and ass with Jesus. c.400

Sometimes Mary lies on a bed with Joseph nearby, while shepherds and Magi approach from either side. Sometimes Mary holds Jesus on her knee, perhaps showing him to the kings or nursing him. The Magi, are usually attired as men from the east in Persian or Syrian dress, sometimes riding horses or camels.

Fig 6: Mary presents Jesus to the three Magi with their camels. One points to the star. A 4th century Roman sarcophagus from St Agnes in Rome

Fig 7: The Magi follow the star. A Byzantine mosaic in Sant' Apollinaire Nuovo in Ravenna, dating to the early 7th century. This is the earliest known occurrence of names for the Magi. Photo by Nina Aldin Thune

As the Roman Empire in the West crumbled, the Byzantine art form of icons and mosaics predominated throughout the Christian church, including parts of Italy which remained under Byzantine rule. In the 6th century the Eastern church promoted the idea of Jesus as God coming to Earth at the Nativity and he is seen with the Virgin who is sitting upright as if giving birth had been no trouble (as St Jerome had said). Christ is sometimes presented as King, and in Carolingian art (named so from Charlemagne, King of the Franks who was crowned as a new West 'Roman' emperor by the pope in 800). He is sometimes shown lying on an altar rather than in a manger, with the cross above foretelling His sacrifice. There are no shepherds or kings.

In the 720s, probably due to the influence of Islam, the Byzantine Emperor Leo III decided that representations of God were blasphemous and should be destroyed. The church, especially Pope Gregory II, disagreed. Pope Gregory was the first native born Roman pope for many years after a long succession of Greeks. After the Roman Empire had fallen in the West, the pope remained in Rome and the papacy gradually asserted its independence from the emperor in Constantinople. Emperor Leo III had tried to impose heavy taxes on Italy to pay for his wars against the Arabs. These two facts and the destruction of images (iconoclasm) were all early nails in the coffin of the relationship between East and West.

The arguments about depictions of God tore the Byzantine Empire apart for 120 years. When it was eventually settled in favour of images, it came with two main caveats. Firstly, only two-dimensional images, icons, were allowed, so the three-dimensional crib or Nativity scene has no place in the Orthodox church. Secondly, the icons themselves were regarded as 'holy' to such an extent that designs remained very similar and there is no stylistic development in the art. Today's icons look almost identical to those painted a thousand years ago.

In contrast, in the Western Church, as early as the 7th century, a council decreed that Christ in his Passion should be depicted as human, and this idea of God being wholly man (as well as wholly God) affected the early Medieval depiction of the Nativity scene. Tenderness towards the Christ child came to the fore. Mary lay (exhausted!) on a couch while Jesus rested in his manger looked over by the ox and ass with Joseph nearby.

Fig 8: Nativity scene from the 12th century Winchester Bible in Winchester Cathedral Library

In both Byzantine and Western art at this time, the midwives are also frequently depicted, often washing the baby in a separate scene. Angels appear in the heavens, sometimes holding up the star. The magi are now definitely depicted with one being ancient and one being black as per the Nativity dramas in the liturgy. They are also usually transformed into kings, rather than wise men from the east. This was perhaps an easier concept for the viewer to grasp, as well as for the artist to depict. The wealthy kings counterbalance the poor shepherds, signifying that Christ came for us all.

Also influenced by the liturgy come the shepherds, either with flower garlands in their hair like classical shepherds, or in hoods and cloaks like contemporary herdsmen, some playing flutes and pipes. In large scenes the Epiphany is sometimes shown separately, as are scenes of the

Fig 9: Byzantine icon showing old, young and black Magi, now crowned as kings, on the middle left, and the two midwives washing Jesus at bottom right, 15th century. Byzantine Museum, Athens

Fig 10: Mosaic of the Nativity in Hosios Loukas Monastery in Greece dating to the early 11th century. Notice the shepherd on the right playing a flute, the Magi on the left and the midwives bathing Baby Jesus.

Annunciation, when the Angel Gabriel told Mary what was to happen; the Visitation, when she visited her cousin Elizabeth who was pregnant with John the Baptist; the Massacre of the Innocents; and the Flight into Egypt.

CHAPTER THREE

St Francis of Assisi to the Reformation

The Life of Francis

Francesco Bernadone, the son of a wealthy draper, was born at Assisi in Italy in c.1181. After an early life of fun and frivolity, he gradually matured following a bout of sickness and the experience of civil war in the area. When he was twenty-six, he heard the voice of God in the church at San Damiano asking him to 'repair my falling house'. Francis thought this meant the physical building at San Damiano and so he sold a bale of his father's cloth (without asking) and spent the money on church repairs. His father disowned him, and he became a poor preacher, living on handouts.

In 1210, Pope Innocent III organised Francis and eleven companions as a quasi-religious order, the Friars Minor, lesser brothers, who were to live lives of poverty and preaching, rather than living in a monastery like monks. Francis realised at this moment that this preaching life was what God had meant by 'repairing his falling house'. God was referring to the increasing wealth and decadence of

Fig 11: Near contemporary portrait of St Francis of Assisi by Cimabue from the Basilica of St Francis in Assisi. Late 13th Century.

the church. The preaching throughout Italy of the Franciscans brought thousands of recruits to the order and by 1217, it had to be reorganised as a fully recognised religious order, and Franciscans were sent across Europe.

Francis had thought about preaching to the Muslims, and got his chance when he was allowed to accompany the Fifth Crusade in 1219. He travelled with Gautier de Brienne to Damietta in Egypt where, after initial successes, the Crusaders were defeated. Francis was able to preach to Sultan Malik al-Kamil, who gave him gifts which are still preserved at Assisi. The preaching did not have the desired effect of conversion, but Francis was allowed to travel to the Holy Land and visit Jerusalem and Bethlehem, which were still in Muslim hands at this time.

Francis was clearly inspired (if not somewhat overwhelmed) by this visit, which no doubt influenced his actions at Greccio four years later (see below). In 1221 Frances and Cardinal Ugolino (later Pope Gregory IX), revised the rules of the order, reiterating the poverty, humility and evangelical freedom of the friars. In 1224, a year after Greccio, Francis received the stigmata, marks on his body mirroring those received by Jesus Christ at his crucifixion. These caused him considerable discomfort in his final years until he died, still a simple deacon, not a priest, in 1226, aged 45. He was canonised two years later, leaving the Order of Franciscans as his memorial.

St Francis at Greccio

St Francis would have seen images of the Nativity as he grew up and seen the crib and picture of Our Lady set up for the Nativity liturgy with the choir of shepherds. He will also have seen, and must have prayed in, the chapel of Santa Maria Ad Praesepe in Rome, recently restored by popes Innocent III and Honorius III. The visit to the Holy Land, however, was perhaps the real inspiration. Greccio, in the valley of the Rieti in Umbria, had had a Franciscan hermitage there from 1217 and Francis was a frequent visitor, preaching to the local peasants. In 1223 he had had a difficult autumn, finishing the final compilation of the rule of the order, and then travelling to Rome for its approval by Pope Honorius III. This had left him depressed and with a desire to get back to doing things the way he wanted to, which encouraged him to ask the pope whether he could celebrate Christmas this year in a way he thought best, to realise the poverty of Christ in the manger.

A fortnight before Christmas he sent for his friend Giovanni Vellita who was a landowner in Greccio and told him that Greccio was where he wanted to celebrate Christmas. He wanted to represent the birth of Christ in Bethlehem so that everyone could see what he suffered for lack of necessities in that manger, and how he lay there with the ox and the ass. Giovanni went to the hermitage at Greccio and filled a manger with hay. On Christmas night, an ox and ass were also led into the chapel and many people came at the behest of Francis to attend the service. Mass was celebrated on the manger (the manger as altar) and Francis sang and then preached to the people on the Nativity, calling Christ 'the little Baby of Bethlehem'. Giovanni, Francis' friend, was so inspired he had a vision, seeing a lifeless babe in the manger which awoke at the approach of Francis. St Bonaventure, who relates this story, goes on to say: 'nor was this vision untrue, for by the grace of God through his servant, blessed Francis, Christ was awakened in many hearts where formerly He slept'. According to another biographer of Francis, Thomas of Celano, the priest at the mass was overcome with emotion, especially at the sweet singing and preaching of Francis, as were many of the congregation. It was obviously a deeply moving religious experience. Hay from the manger was kept as a souvenir by many and considered to have miraculous powers of healing, especially for women in childbirth and sick animals.

This event at Greccio has been called a Nativity play or the first crib, but it is not really either. Despite Giovanni's vision, it seems unlikely that there was a baby in the crib, either real or a model, especially since the crib was the altar. The ox and ass were there, but there were no shepherds, kings or midwives, or any of the traditional liturgical dialogues discussed earlier. What really happened at Greccio was simply a reimagining of the scene of the Nativity, such as St Jerome had done for himself 800 years before. Francis told the tale from the Gospels and preached to the people in such a way that they imagined themselves there at the time. Indeed, Francis was so absorbed that it has been said that he was no longer in Greccio, but thought himself back in Bethlehem. The lasting significance of Greccio was that it put the celebration of Christmas on a par with that of Easter in the church, and the Franciscans were responsible for spreading this idea and the idea of the crib that went with it.

Followers of St Francis

Two literary works also responsible for this new-found joy in the feast of Christmas were the *Golden Legend* by James of Voragine, written in about 1260, and the *Hundred Meditations on the Life of Christ* written in about 1300. This latter was originally ascribed to St Bonaventure but is now known to have been written by a Franciscan friar, Jacobus de Sancto Geminiano. The *Golden Legend*'s chapter on the Nativity, talks of the miraculous hay in the manger, and of the ox and ass, but it also gives a full version of the story of the Roman Emperor Octavian (Augustus) consulting with the Sybil who shows him a golden sun, in the centre of which is the Virgin and Child. The Sybil explains to the Emperor that the sun is Heaven and the child is greater than he. This story leads to some Italian cribs having figures of the Emperor and the Sybil.

The *Golden Legend* also speaks vividly of the journey of the Magi, following a star in which they see the form of a fair Boy, above whom was a cross, an image which also crossed into art. It probably also inspired the great Magi procession instituted at Milan in the 14th century by the Dominicans. The Magi set out from the Church of Santa Maria delle Grazie to the church of San Lorenzo, where they encountered Herod, and then on to the crib itself at Sant' Eustorgio. They handed over their gifts to Our Lady and Jesus and then moved to another part of the church for the dream scene and their return home.

The *Meditations* proved even more popular. This has a thoroughly Franciscan version of the Nativity. It took a long time, says the book, for Mary to reach Bethlehem, and she and Joseph were so poor that they had to travel with an ox and an ass like so many merchants going to Bethlehem fair. They were so often delayed that all the inns were full when they finally arrived. Joseph found some shelter outside the town (though not apparently a cave) and made a door for it with his carpentry skills. He was sad he could not make things more comfortable. Mary leans against a pillar and gives birth (in ecstasy rather than pain). She washes Jesus with her breast milk, wraps him in her veil and lays him in the manger where the ox and the ass warm him with their breath. She kneels in adoration. The angels sing, and the shepherds visit to adore him. 'Do thou likewise,' says the *Meditations*, 'and ask His Mother that she may give Him to thee to hold and caress within thine arms and look well on His Face and reverently kiss and be glad of Him. And this thou canst

25

do in all confidence, for he has come to dwell among sinners for their salvation.' These words have the genuine ring of St Francis about them.

The *Meditations* then has Jesus being taken to Jerusalem for his circumcision, but returning to Bethlehem in time to greet the Three Kings. Jesus blesses them and sends them on their way, and then Mary and Joseph stay with Jesus by the manger and often hold him and play with him. Every Christian soul is then admonished to not let a day pass during the forty days of Christmas without visiting Our Lady and her Son in the crib. (We would say twenty-eight days of Advent and twelve days of Christmas.) The success of the *Meditations* was enormous. It was read all over Europe and rapidly translated from the Latin into the vernacular, be it English, French, German etc.

Another follower of St Francis was St Bridget of Sweden (1303–1373) whose *Revelations* come across as a distinct vision rather than the excited imaginations of the *Meditations*: 'When I was present by the manger of the Lord in Bethlehem, I beheld a Virgin of extreme beauty well wrapped in a white mantle and a delicate tunic through which I clearly perceived her virgin body. With her was an old man of great honesty, and they brought with them an ox and ass. These entered the cave, and the man after having tied them to the manger went outside and brought to the Virgin a burning candle, and having attached this to the wall, he went outside again so that he might not be present at the birth.

'Then the Virgin pulled off the shoes from her feet, drew off the white mantle that enveloped her, removed the veil from her head, laying it by her side, thus remaining in her tunic alone, with her beautiful golden hair falling loosely over her shoulders. Then she produced two small linen cloths and two woollen ones of exquisite purity and fineness which she had brought to wrap up the Child who was to be born, and two other small pieces with which to cover and bind His Head, and these she put down beside her in order to use them in due time. And when all was thus prepared the Virgin knelt down with great veneration in an attitude of prayer and her back was turned to the manger, but her face was lifted up to Heaven, turned towards the east. Thus, with her hands extended and her eyes fixed on the sky, she was standing as in an ecstasy, lost in contemplation, in a rapture of divine sweetness.

'And while she was standing thus in prayer I saw the Child in her womb move; suddenly in a moment she gave birth to her own Son, from whom radiated such an ineffable light and splendour that the sun was not comparable to it, nor did the candle which Saint Joseph put there give any light, the divine light totally annihilating the material light of the candle. And so sudden and instantaneous was this way of bringing forth that I could neither discover nor discern how or by means of what member she gave birth. Verily, though all of a sudden, I saw the glorious Infant lying on the ground naked and shining. His body was pure from any kind of soil or impurity. Then I heard also the singing of the angels which was of miraculous sweetness and great beauty. When therefore the Virgin felt that she had already borne her Child, immediately she worshipped Him, her hands clasped with honour and great reverence, and said to Him: "Be welcome my God, my Lord, my Son."

'Then as the Child was whining and trembling from the cold and the hardness of the floor where He was lying, He stretched out His arms, imploring her to raise Him to the warmth of her motherly love. So the Mother took Him in her arms and pressed Him to her breast, and with her cheek and breast she warmed Him with great joy and tender maternal compassion. She then sat down on the ground, laying the Child on her lap, and at once she began to bestow on Him much care, tying up His small body, His legs and arms with long cloths. Then she enveloped the head of the Child in two linen garments prepared for the purpose, and when this was done the old man entered, and prostrating himself on the floor he wept for joy. And in no way was the Virgin changed by birth, neither as to the colour of her face nor as to any illness, and her bodily strength did not decline, as is usually the case with women when they bear. But then she stood up, and together the two, that is herself and Joseph, put Him in the manger and on their knees worshipped Him with immense joy until the arrival of the Kings, and the Kings recognised the Son from His likeness to His Mother.'

Another mystic to mention here is Margery Kempe from King's Lynn in Norfolk. She was born in c.1373, the year St Bridget died, and she travelled widely on pilgrimage in her later life, visiting Rome (where she met people who had known Bridget) and Assisi. In the Holy Land she too had a vision of the Nativity: 'And then the creature [Margery] went forth with Our Lady to Bethlehem and procured lodgings for her every night with great reverence, and Our Lady was received with good cheer. She also begged for Our Lady pieces of fair white cloth and kerchiefs to swaddle her Son in when He was born; and when Jesus was born she arranged bedding for Our Lady to lie on with Her blessed Son. And later she begged food for Our Lady and her blessed Child. Afterwards she swaddled Him, weeping bitter tears of compassion, mindful of the painful death He would suffer for love of sinful men, saying to Him: "Lord, I shall treat You gently; I will not bind You tightly. I pray you not to be displeased with me." And afterwards on the twelfth day, when Three Kings came with their gifts and worshipped Our Lord Jesus Christ in his mother's lap, this creature, Our Lady's handmaiden, beholding the whole process in contemplation, wept marvellously sorely.'

Margery, like Bridget, had been a mother before choosing a religious life, officially in Bridget's case, unofficially in Margaret's, and so they both knew what childbirth was really like. Bridget's account is striking in that we have a painless, miraculous birth, as envisioned by St Jerome, and that Mary kneels before Jesus rather than lying down on a bed, giving us the image of so many crib scenes since. The light coming from the Christ child is frequently shown in art after this time but hard to manage in a crib. It is however the reason Joseph is sometimes depicted holding a lantern. It is from Bridget's vision that so many Marys are depicted with blonde hair, a Swedish idea of beauty rather than a Middle Eastern one perhaps, but it is the beauty of Our Lady that is important, her inner beauty especially. In Margery's account we have her taking St Francis very literally and being with Mary on her journey, paying the bills for her and organising the swaddling! It is probable that Margery is inspired by the story of the midwives and imagines herself at the crib in the place of one of them.

The First Cribs

In the *Meditations*, we saw that people were enjoined to visit the crib every day in the Christmas season and so the crib in its earliest form begins to appear. There must have been one at Assisi as St Clare imagines herself being there when she is ill. She hears the organ and the friars chanting and she sees the crib of the Lord. There is also mention of a crib at the Klosterkirche in Füssen in Germany near the Austrian border. Rudolf von Thulhofen left money for an eternal light for the crib there in 1252, only a generation after Greccio. We know that an early crib was given by Sanchia, wife of Robert of Anjou (king of Naples), to the church of St

Clare in Naples sometime after 1311, which apparently had the manger as an altar with an ox and ass to each side, and Mary and Joseph behind.

When the Holy Land finally came under Muslim control at the end of the 13th century, the body of St Jerome was translated from Bethlehem to be buried under the altar of the Praesepe chapel in Maria Maggiore in Rome. It was at this time that the silver reliquary was created for the remains of the manger and then the earliest surviving crib group, with life-sized figures, was created by Arnolfo di Cambio to stand behind the altar. We are uncertain of the exact original layout since there have been some restorations since, and the whole group was moved into the crypt in the 16th century. The statue of Our Lady was replaced at this time, perhaps because the original was damaged in the move. This statue and the other statues of the group have been cleaned and restored and they are now in the museum of the cathedral.

Fig 12: Nativity Group by Arnolfo di Cambio, 1291,
Maria Maggiore Museum

The remaining figures show Joseph and the Three Kings as well as half figures of the ox and ass. It seems likely that these were inserted into some form of stable so a back half was not required, or perhaps they stood behind the manger with a wall behind. The original scene would probably have had shepherds and angels, but it is uncertain whether Jesus himself was shown in Mary's arms in the original statue or not. Maybe the replacement Mary was carved because previously Jesus had not been shown and now the church wanted to show him in Mary's arms, or perhaps before he had had his own baby statue which was lost or damaged at some point. We simply don't know. What is certain is that these statues were a permanent fixture in the Praesepe chapel and were not brought out just for Christmas.

Fig 13: Wooden Nativity group from the 1290s in the Martyrium of Santo Stefano in Bologna

The only other crib which can lay claim to such an early date is that housed in the Martyrium of the Church of Santo Stefano in Bologna. Restoration work in the 1980s established that these figures were carved from lime and elm wood by the 'Master of the Crucifix' also in Bologna, which is dated to 1291. These wooden Nativity figures (also life-sized) are thus contemporary with Arnolfo's crib. The surviving figures show Mary presenting Baby Jesus alongside Joseph and the Three Kings. There may once have been an ox and ass, since lost, but it is interesting that there are no shepherds here either. Having kings but not shepherds may be a continuation of an earlier tradition when Epiphany was considered the most important part of the Christmas season, or perhaps the sculptor was simply following the Gospel of Matthew religiously and there never were shepherds or an ox and ass. The figures were presumably painted originally, but the painting and gilding we have today is by Simone dei Crocifissi and dates from 1370.

Other references to early cribs are few and far between, and survivors of figures from before the Reformation rarer still. Before we look at these, we must now turn to the Medieval mystery plays and the contemporary art to get an impression of how these cribs may have appeared.

The Nativity Plays

After a hiatus following papal disapproval of plays, Nativity plays flourished again towards the end of the 14th century, usually with actors, but occasionally with puppets. It seems the word marionette comes from Mary; the first marionettes being 'little Marys' for use in both Nativity and passion plays. The plays began life as an adjunct to the sermon (as had happened before) and were performed in the vernacular rather than Latin, by the clergy or members of a guild. These plays soon grew in elaboration and took ideas from the *Meditations* and the work of artists, and the writers were also inspired by their own imaginations. Cradles made for these plays became particularly elaborate either with gothic canopies, or on rockers, or even made of silver (see Fig 14). This cradle would be rocked in Christmas services, and lullabies sung to send Jesus to sleep. Some families would have their own cradle which they would bring to church to rock at the appropriate time, while in the Béguinages of Flanders (houses of lay religious women, not nuns) it was common for the Béguines to each have a cradle in their cell in which they kept a wax Baby Jesus, for whom they made clothes and coverlets as an act of worship during the Christmas period. It was probably around this time that a particular English custom developed of making savoury mince pies shaped as cradles to eat during the Christmas season. These mince pies were banned by Oliver Cromwell in the 17th century and, when they were reintroduced, they were sweet and round and had lost their religious connotations.

There is a Nativity play attributed to Gautier de Coincy (1177–1236) which is based on the apocryphal Gospel of James, on stories of St Bridget and on other imaginings. In this play the story is told with all the zest of the tales of King Arthur or the 'Song of Roland'. It tells how all the animals came to worship the Christ Child and that the ox and ass refrained from eating any straw that night so that Mary might have a soft

31

Fig 14: Elaborate rocking cradle from c.1500, attributed to Jan Borman II,
Rijksmuseum, Amsterdam

bed for Jesus. The author remarks: 'How many oxen and asses I know, dressed in the finest silk and cloth, how many oxen and asses I know who would not have done the like.'

The Nativity plays could be very long, passing through every part of the story from the Annunciation to the Flight into Egypt. Some scenes were strictly devotional, but others lapsed into noisy revels. The ass now became a major feature, bearing Mary to the church service where the congregation would make the responses by braying! The scene at the inn became very rowdy with no room for Mary and Joseph amidst a crowd of revellers.

In the English plays Joseph spends much of his time riven with doubt about Mary's pregnancy, but this theme does not appear in the plays on the continent. The two midwives appear on the continent and in England, where they are named Salome and Zelomye in the Coventry *Nativity* play. Sometimes Mary and Joseph have a maid who also appears in some surviving continental plays. In the Coventry play, *Joseph*, she is called Susanna. In France, the kings would be loaded down with Flanders cloth, Burgundy grapes, truffles, or whatever other extravagant presents could be brought to the scene, as well as the gold, frankincense and myrrh. Spanish mystery plays for the Nativity were more serious affairs than the French, where Our Lady was presented as Queen of Heaven with a halo of stars and the kings were quietly reverent. Everywhere, much was made of the kings' train of followers.

At the crib scene, shepherds would bring gifts as well as the kings. In the York plays these gifts were a spruce box, a ball and a bottle, or cherries, a bird and a ball, or again, a pipe, a hat and mittens. The cherries are a clue as to when the plays were performed. In England, the Nativity plays were often shown in the summer, after Corpus Christi, rather than at Christmas itself. Unlike Italy and elsewhere on the continent, the shepherds are not generally named in England, although Mak and his wife appear in *The Second Shepherds Play* from the Towneley series of Wakefield. In this play the shepherds put a stolen lamb in a cradle and try to pass it off as a baby and then proceed to advise Mary on the art of child rearing! In Tuscany the shepherds are named Nencio, Bobi and Randello. Nencio won't search for the Saviour until he has had breakfast and then he needs to bring his boy along and then the dogs Giordano and Falconello! Their gifts to the Baby are a sack of wood, cheeses and chestnuts, and a flute, bought at Bethlehem Fair. Gifts are received by a benevolent St Joseph who only wants two cheeses! Back in Tuscany the shepherds meet the kings and the midwives who, with their children, Abramo and Samuelino, are off to see Herod. The mother of one child won't allow him to speak to the other and it ends up in a rowdy street scene enlivened by a crowd of beggars who have been following the kings! We see how far the plays had come from devotional re-enactments in church.

Protests against the plays were heard at the Council of Basle from 1431 to 1449, and by the end of the century it was made clear that the church was no place for such performances. Any dramas in church were to be strictly devotional, while the excesses of the plays went into secular halls or the great outdoors. In the 16th century, Luther's Protestant Reformation put an end to plays in northern Europe, and the Roman Catholic Council of Trent (1545–1563) re-enforced the ban on such plays being held in churches. In England, the writers struggled to adapt the plays to the new Protestantism and were forced to give up; the plays were performed for the last time at Coventry in 1580. They have only been recently revived in England with a performance at a York pageant in 1909 and then regular performances at York since 1951, following the Festival of Britain. Since 1989 there has been an annual Nativity play held at Wintershall in Surrey, which gives a good impression of what a 14th century play would have been like, though of the devotional kind rather than the sensational.

Fig 15: A scene from the Wintershall Nativity Play of 2016

The Crib in Art Before the Reformation

Though the plays left the churches and eventually disappeared, the crib remained and it is time to look at the contemporary art of *c.*1220 to 1500 to see what it can tell us about how cribs may have appeared in churches during this time, especially as it is known that many artists were also responsible for the scenery and decorations of the Nativity plays. Pisa Cathedral in north Italy is an excellent place to start since it features two Nativity scenes carved by Nicola Pisano (1220/5–c.1284) and his son Giovanni (c.1250–c.1315). The contrast between the two is great. Nicola learned his craft by studying classical sculptures, and it shows. The layout is traditional with Mary lying down after giving birth and midwives washing Jesus below, and with shepherds to the right. But his Mary looks up Heavenwards with pride like a pagan goddess, virtually ignoring the baby in the manger.

Fig 16: Nativity scene from the baptistry pulpit in Pisa Cathedral by Nicola Pisano, c.1266.

The difference seen fifty years later in Giovanni's Nativity scene is telling. The overall layout is the same but the figures here are full of tenderness and humanity. One of the midwives is testing the water to check it is the right temperature for the baby. Mary lies next to, and is totally absorbed by, the Baby Jesus. She tenderly lifts his covers to show us our Saviour.

In the 14th century this traditional layout, derived from Byzantine models, starts to disappear. French ivories and Nottingham alabaster representations of the 14th century generally follow the Byzantine iconography of a recumbent Mary. Fig 18 shows Mary in a 14th century bed, with Jesus in the cot by her side and a single midwife or maid to help.

Fig 17: Nativity scene from the main pulpit in Pisa Cathedral by Giovanni Pisano, c.1305

Fig 18: Nottingham alabaster Nativity, c.1400

Fig 19: Nativity *by Giotto in the Scrovegni Chapel, Padua, c.1305*

Fig 20: Nativity with Isaiah and Ezekiel *by Duccio di Buoninsegna in Siena Cathedral Museum, 1308–1311*

In his painting (Fig 19), Giotto has both a shed and a cave, although Our Lady still reclines on her bed whilst angels dance on the shed roof and shepherds attend. In his *Nativity* at Siena (Fig 20), Duccio combines shed and cave in much the same way, with midwives and shepherds. But there are also panels on either side featuring Isaiah and Ezekiel, prophets of the coming of Jesus. Some later three-dimensional cribs contain two prophets along with shepherds and kings. More often in the art of this period, Mary is shown sitting, often with Jesus on her lap being nursed, or simply being shown to us or to the Magi or kings. The scenes from the mystery plays intrude with shepherds dancing with shepherdesses or playing with their dogs. The kings are shown in great triumphal processions, such as those we have mentioned taking place in Milan as part of the play cycles.

Fig 21: The Epiphany *by Gentile in the Uffizi Museum. 1420–1423*

Fig 22: The Nativity *by Gentile in the Uffizi Museum. 1420–1423*

Fig 23: The Flight into Egypt *by Gentile in the Uffizi Museum. 1420–1423*

Gentile's masterpiece, *The Epiphany*, in the Uffizi shows Jesus on Mary's lap being shown to the kings, who are dressed as contemporary Renaissance princes with horses and a splendid retinue which tails off into the distance. The two midwives stand at the left. Below this panel are two smaller pictures, one of the Nativity itself, where the midwives have fallen asleep and Mary is kneeling to worship Jesus in a scene from the vision of St Bridget, and the Flight into Egypt, where the Holy Family seems to be saying goodbye to the two midwives, who will indeed soon be left out of crib history. These two smaller panels are noteworthy for their backgrounds. The world into which Jesus comes is a beautiful one. It is a starry night on the mountains where the angels appear to the shepherds. On the Flight into Egypt scene, flowering trees and little hilltop towns decorate the landscape.

The influence of St Bridget begins to be seen in the inclusion of a pillar against which Our Lady leant to give birth, or Joseph's candle is shown. Sometimes the pillar becomes part of a ruined classical temple complex in which the Nativity is set, showing the death of the classical world at the birth of the Christian. In case the humanity of God intrudes too much, nativities begin to be shown with Our Lady kneeling before Jesus to remind us of his divinity. Ghirlandio's *Nativity* has Jesus' manger as a classical trough, with Mary and the shepherds kneeling before him. The Magi are on their way in the distance. Foppa also shows the Nativity in a temple with a pillar for Mary to lean on, and the Magi worshipping.

Boticelli's *Nativity* shows a kneeling Mary along with a small kneeling John the Baptist. The latter, Jesus' cousin and forerunner, occasionally makes his way into these crib scenes, sometimes playing games with the boy shepherds.

Fig 24: The Nativity in a ruined temple *by Ghirlandaio in the Basilica di Santa Trinita, Florence, c.1485*

Fig 25: The Adoration of the Kings *by Vincenzo Foppa, active in 1456, showing the Nativity in a ruined temple*

Fig 26: The Nativity *by Sandro Boticelli (c.1445–1510)*
showing a kneeling Mary

In the 15th century, church decoration moves from frescoes and pulpits to the great altar screens and the altars and retables themselves. There is the great screen in Chartres in France with over 200 figures depicting the life of Christ, and the carved and sometimes painted altars of Germany and Flanders, particularly from the Tyrol, which were often called Bethlehems.

The Nativity altar by Hans Klocher in Bolzano shows Mary and Joseph worshipping Jesus. There are further scenes on the doors which would normally be kept closed except on special feast days. As a Nativity altar, it seems likely that these doors were only opened for the Christmas season. This would in turn lead to the idea of cribs coming out only at Christmas, rather than being visible all year round as in the earlier large statue groups.

The Tramin altar, also by Klocher, has a similar layout but with angels within the crib scene, and the ox and ass and shepherds (dressed in contemporary clothes) looking through the windows. In the background,

Fig 27: Nativity altar by Hans Klocher in Bolzano, South Tyrol, c.1500

Fig 28: The Tramin altar by Hans Klocher, Bavarian National Museum,
Munich, 1485-90

the kings can be seen approaching. Another panel by Klocher or a close follower, sold by Christies Auctions, New York, in the 1990s, is one of the first to show one of the kings as being black, also following the mystery plays, usually the king named Melchior.

Fig 29: Nativity altar by Veit Stoss in Bamberg Cathedral, 1523

Veit Stoss, who made the marvellous triptych in St Mary's Church in Krakow (which has small Nativity scenes on the side panels) also made a Nativity altar for Nuremburg which is now housed in Bamberg Cathedral. This altar is unpainted and features a large (St Bridget's) pillar in the middle of the scene. The four further scenes on the doors here are the Flight into Egypt, Mary's birth, the Epiphany, and Jesus in the temple as a child.

Whilst German altars concentrated on the shepherds and the family life of Jesus, those of Italy and Spain preferred the ostentation of the Three Kings' arrival. Spanish retables are more elaborate than German and were also called Bethlehems. One Spanish word for a crib today is derived from this, a Belen. There is an excellent example at Burgos with Mary presenting Jesus to the kings, one of whom is black. Jesus is in a playful mood and wants to examine his presents. This central panel is polychromed and gilded wood, with the doors bearing painted scenes from the life of Christ.

Fig 30: Triptych of the Epiphany *by the Master of Covarrubias at Covarrubias near Burgos, northern Spain, early 16ᵗʰ century*

Fig 31: Nativity with St Francis and St Anthony *by Luca and Andrea della Robbia in the Chapel of Santa Maria degli Angeli at La Verna, c.1490s*

In Italy, pride of place goes to the majolica altars of Luca and Andrea Della Robbia. Many of their works were carried out for the Franciscans and promoted Franciscan ideals of the Holy Family. Their example at La Verna (built on the site where St Francis received the stigmata) shows the heavenly host of angels above a simple manger, presumably in a cave, although it could even be outside. Mary and Joseph kneel either side and next to them stand the two great Franciscan saints, St Francis of Assisi himself and St Anthony of Padua.

The slightly later altar by Andrea, now in the Victoria and Albert Museum, London, shows Our Lady presenting Jesus to the Magi, this time with a stable crib in the background and a long procession of the kings' entourage stretching into the background. After 1500, Giovanni Della

Fig 32: Adoration of the Magi *by Andrea della Robbia, c.1500*

Robbia started to fashion figures in the round with painted backgrounds and it soon became popular to have terracotta or plaster figure groups, generally life-size, set up in a chapel. Franciscan convents were especially keen on setting up a series of shrines or chapels on a wooded hill as a place of pilgrimage. These 'Sacred Mountains' were usually arranged like the landscape of Jerusalem, where pilgrims could follow the life of Christ without having the expense and difficulty of visiting the Holy Land. Moving through these chapels of life-size scenes was rather like a still mystery play. The earliest Sacred Mountain is probably that at San Vivaldo in Tuscany, where there was a Franciscan hermitage dating from the 13th century. The twenty-five chapels here date from 1500 to 1516 and contain a mixture of wooden and terracotta statues, some by the Della Robbia family, but there is no Nativity here despite there being later Annunciation and Flight into Egypt chapels.

Fig 33: Adoration of the Shepherds Chapel, Varallo, 16th century

A much more ambitious Sacred Mountain is at Varallo in Piedmont, where there are forty-five chapels, including eleven dedicated to the Nativity cycle. The Massacre of the Innocents Chapel has no less than seventy life-size figures. Although some parts of this Sacred Mountain originally dated from 1491, the whole layout was revamped in the later 16th century following the Counter Reformation.

Early Statue Groups and Cribs

Even before these chapel groups of figures in the sacred mountains, similar large Nativity groups were being commissioned for churches, made up of separate, usually life-size figures.

Fig 34: Nativity *in painted terracotta by Guido Mazzoni in the crypt of Modena Cathedral, 1480s*

Fig 35: Nativity *by Begarelli in Modena Cathedral, 1527*

The Cathedral at Modena has two Nativity groups from this period. That by Mazzoni consists of four surviving life-size statues including Our Lady with Jesus on her lap, who is about to be fed some broth by a maidservant (midwife?) who is blowing on the spoon to cool it. The other two figures are a contemporarily dressed peasant (possibly Joseph, or Joachim, Mary's father) and a woman in more biblical attire, possibly Mary's mother, St Anne. They are made of polychromed terracotta. The smaller crib by Begarelli, also terracotta, depicts the Nativity in a cave, and is much more elaborate, with no less than eight shepherds dressed in classical style looking on.

Some of these statue groups or early cribs were also now being ordered by private families for their own households. We know that the Dukes of Milan set up their own crib in the late 15th century and, in the 1520s, the 15-year-old Buontalenti made a crib for the son of Cosimo de Medici, first Grand Duke of Tuscany. It is a pity this does not survive, as it was apparently the first automaton Nativity. Clouds descended and angels flew, and the figures marched towards the crib in a grand procession.

Although there are no mentions of such early pre-Reformation cribs in England, there are mentions in Germany and some evidence for France and Flanders. In 1491 there is a record that Meister Ulrich made a Nativity group for the Duchess Kunegunde in Bavaria, and there are small 15th century clay figures found in the Moselle region and Westphalia.

Fig 36: Clay crib figures of Mary and a king, from Germany, mid-16th century (Author's collection)

The author has two clay figures from Germany, Mary and a king which, although slightly later in date, show the simplicity of these figures. Cast in moulds (the king is 10.5cm tall), the figures would probably originally have been painted. There is no sign of paint on these two pieces because they were recovered from a dump. Although they seem well-formed, they had been thrown away (along with a great many others), possibly in connection with the Reformation. They show that by the late 15th century, any family household, not just the wealthy, could put together a crib scene in their house.

Fig 37: Surviving figures of a Nativity by Pietro and Giovanni Alemanno in Naples Museum, 1478

In Italy, Naples begins to emerge as a centre of crib manufacture. In 1458, Alberico Meroballis commissioned Martino de Simone da Jadena to carve eleven crib figures for Sant' Agostino Maggiore, and in 1478 Jacomello Pepi, scent-maker to the Duke of Calabria, ordered a crib from Pietro and Giovanni Alemanno, for the Church of San Giovanni dei Carbonari in Naples. This crib originally had forty-eight figures, including Baby Jesus, a crowned Our Lady, Joseph, ox and ass, three shepherds, twelve sheep, two dogs, four trees, eleven angels, two prophets and two sybils. The large number of figures means this group is often considered to be the first 'proper' crib, where three dimensional figures could be moved around (and lost or broken!). They are slightly smaller than life-size. The twelve surviving figures show what an amazing sight it must have been when it was all there. The Tyrol and Naples both claim the first position in the history and manufacture of cribs, so it is lovely that these figures were made in Naples by brothers from the Tyrol, thus pleasing both camps.

Fig 38: Nativity by Giovanni de Nola in Santa Maria del Porto in Naples, 1520–1525

Another slightly later crib or statue group is that by Giovanni de Nola for Santa Maria del Porto (Our Lady of Childbirth) in Naples. These life-size wooden figures show Mary, Joseph and three shepherds (the baby is a later replacement) but there were originally many more, and time has not been kind to the survivors. Another crib by de Nola had Mary, Joseph and Jesus on an upper-level stable with shepherds and beasts in a cave below.

In 1507, Pietro Belverte of Bergamo was commissioned by the church of San Domenico Maggiore in Naples for a crib of 28 figures which were to be placed in a grotto made of stones brought from Bethlehem itself. Only Mary, Joseph, the ox and the ass survive.

From Naples, the idea of free-standing Nativity scenes spread to Spain. After all, they were all part of the same kingdom then. There are some surviving figures from a set at Palma in Mallorca thought to have been made by the Alemanno family. The Mary, Joseph and some of the angels are late 15th century but the Baby Jesus is a later replacement. Mary and Joseph are a very serious couple. There is none of the joy or playfulness of the German cribs, but perhaps the now missing shepherds and kings would have told us a different story.

Fig 39: Surviving figures of Pietro Belverte's Nativity in San Domenico Maggiore in Naples, 1507–1511

Fig 40: Spanish Nativity (Belen) at La Sang Church, Palma in Mallorca, late 15th century

These multifigured Nativity scenes, especially those of Italy, have come a long way from the simple re-enactment of Jesus' birth by St Francis at Greccio. But, if we go back to the original Nativity where Mary and Joseph arrive in Bethlehem and are unable to find any room at the inn, Bethlehem must have been a busy and bustling place. And it is the busy and the bustling which will define the cribs of the 16th and later centuries.

CHAPTER FOUR

The Reformation and the Rise of the Crib

Reformation and Counter Reformation

The Protestant reformation insisted that religious belief should be based on what was written in the Bible and that no notice should be taken of the apocryphal works, like the Apocryphal Gospel of James, nor of various church traditions which had no basis in the Bible. For the most part, Protestantism was also rather set against statues, particularly of Our Lady and the saints, seeing the sin of idolatry there. The crib was under threat. The Catholic Church could see that the Protestant reformers had some good points. There had always been mainstream doubts about some aspects of the Nativity plays, for example. St Charles Borromeo, a leading light in the Catholic Counter Reformation argued against them, and they were banned in France in 1547. Protestant reformers themselves banned puppet plays in England and burnt the puppets in London in 1538. Catholic Spain banned puppet plays in 1600 but plays with real people continued there and in many other countries.

The Catholic Council of Trent in 1545 denounced the use of moveable figures in church services, probably as a counter to the Protestant argument that people were deceived by accounts of miraculous moving statues. In art too, where Protestants whitewashed the medieval frescoes in churches, the reform movement had an effect. In paintings, the depiction of the Nativity becomes simpler. Apocryphal scenes from the mystery plays are omitted (we say a final goodbye to the two midwives) and we are left with the Virgin Mary kneeling before the manger with Joseph and the shepherds. The ox and ass are occasionally left out and even the kings are not always shown, lest they remind the viewer of extravagant church processions and plays.

This austerity was short-lived however. Whilst some Protestant sects became more extreme, with Swiss Protestants under Zwingli burning every statue they could find and, later, with joyless puritans under Cromwell even banning the celebration of Christmas in England, the leading lights of the Counter Reformation decided on a fight back.

In 1517, the year that Luther pinned his theses to the church door in Wittenberg and the Reformation gathered pace, Cajetan (Gaetano), later St Cajetan, attended a mass in the Presepio Chapel of St Maria Maggiore in Rome, just a year after his ordination. There he had a vision of Mary placing Baby Jesus in his arms, followed by further visions of Christ's infancy, which inspired him to preach frequently on the subject. Cajetan was one of many men who sought to counter the Reformation with better trained clergy. In 1524 with Bishop John Peter Caraffa (later Pope Paul IV) he founded the religious order of the Theatines, who would devote themselves especially to bible study. Other important reformers at this time were St Philip Neri, founder of the Congregation of the Oratory, and St Ignatius Loyola, founder of the Society of Jesus (Jesuits), who celebrated his first mass at the Presepio Chapel in St Maria Maggiore. Another important figure was Pope Sixtus V (pope 1585–1590). A Franciscan and a great reformer who encouraged the Jesuits, especially in the promotion of the faith in Poland, he also embarked on many building projects. One of these was moving the Presepio Chapel to its present position in St Maria Maggiore and presenting it with a new crib. Pope Sixtus also canonised Bonaventure which encouraged renewed interest in his *Meditations*.

Naples

Following St Cajetan's vision in the Presepio Chapel, he always set up a crib for the celebration of Christmas and invited local shepherds to come and play their bagpipes at the crib. Although this tradition began in Rome, war forced Cajetan and the Theatines to move south to Naples in 1526. There he was shocked by the poverty he saw, and did his utmost to relieve the situation, even founding a chain of pawnbrokers, not run for profit, but simply to help those in financial difficulty. He also now saw a major problem with the ideas of the Protestant reformers. If pictures, statues and plays are removed, and faith only comes from the Bible, that is of little use to those unable to read. He and his fellow Catholic reformers saw that the crib was an excellent way of promoting the faith and for telling the people that when Jesus was born he was poor, just like them. In 1533, the Theatines under Cajetan set up a Nativity in their new church of Santa Maria della Stalla (St Mary of the Stable) in Naples. The people of Naples took to the crib like a duck to water. The Neapolitans loved festivals and the theatre, still mostly connected to the church, and they saw the crib as another reason to celebrate. It became an escape from the poverty of their lives, sometimes literally as many turned to making crib figures to support themselves. By the end of the 16th century, crib making was a defined trade in Naples, carried out by artists called Figurari, who set up in the Vico dei Figurari, where they still make cribs and crib figures today.

Encouraged by Cajetan and the Theatines, the Neapolitan crib swiftly leaves behind the simplicity of the crib of St Francis to incorporate a grand picture of Neapolitan life. Jesus came for us all, so all life is represented there, from all sections of society. The Duchess of Amalfi had a crib made for her in Naples, some time before 1567, which contained 167 figures, including many scenes featuring shepherds, and a large and elaborate retinue for the Magi. This is generally considered to be the first privately owned crib in Naples. By the early 17th century, Neapolitan cribs were being sold abroad, particularly in Spain, and some Neapolitans even travelled abroad to sell their wares. Dozens of makers are known by their names including Francesco Picano, Lorenzo Vaccaro, Aniello Falcone, and the Bottiglieri brothers, Ceraso and Somma (the latter known as the Donatello dei Pastori). Also in the 17th century, cribs for private houses become more common, with rich Neapolitans trying to outdo each other in their splendour and numbers of figures. Now also began the practice of putting cribs out just for the Christmas season and then packing them away until the next year.

These early figures were generally made of plaster or wood, and painted. In the 17th century, Vaccaro made a set of life-size wooden figures for the church of Santa Maria in Portico, which were dressed in real clothes. This led to a greater attempt at realism amongst the Figurari. The figures, usually about 30 cm tall, began to be made, like puppets, on a wire armature with heads, hands and feet made of stucco, wood or terracotta.

These figures could be arranged in a variety of positions and were dressed in clothes made of material. Because of their relationship to puppets, they are often called puppets (pupazzi) in Naples, as well as *pastori* which can mean any of the figures, except the Holy Family, not just the shepherds. The Holy Family (Jesus, Mary and Joseph) is referred to as *il mistero* (the mystery), a term from the mystery plays. The grandest nativities in private homes were often arranged by theatre directors and could be opened to the public with accompanying musical recitals. The Neapolitan tradition of cribs would expand greatly in the 18th century but let us first see how cribs developed elsewhere in the 16th and 17th centuries.

Sicily and Italy

In a similar way to Naples, the crib flourished elsewhere in Sicily and Italy from the 16th century, with cribs in every church and owned by various confraternities who organised (and still organise) grand processions on festival days. In Palermo there is a Via Bambinai (Baby Street or Doll Street) where the crib makers made their figures. Sicilians, like Neapolitans, had some jointed figures, but they preferred those carved from one piece of wood, generally lime wood, or made from terracotta. Linen material for clothes was often dipped in gesso so it could be moulded as required and then painted. This gesso was a warm glue saturated with chalk which bonded to the wooden figure and made realistic pleats and flowing garments. The figures are full of movement and sometimes a little windswept. The early figures are generally smaller than those of Naples. The Jesuits encouraged the making of cribs in Sicily when they erected a large Nativity scene on the stage of the Mamertine College in Messina in 1609. This stage had been the scene of the first production of a play by Jesuit students in 1551, and Jesuit colleges continue to promote drama, both secular and religious.

The best known of the early Sicilian crib makers was Giovanni Matera (1653–1718), whose figures are miniature masterpieces of sculpture, even if a whole scene full of them can be rather overwhelming. He was based at Trapani, which became an early centre for crib making. The makers at Trapani specialised in mountain scenes, and also developed the use of expensive materials such as lava stone mountains set with trees made of red coral. The figures themselves could be made of ivory for the wealthy end of the market.

Fig 41: Crib figure *by Giovanni Matera made of wood and papier mâché, c.1700*

Fig 42: Nativity from Trapani at Compton Verney House, made of silver and coral, c.1700

There is an excellent example of a Trapani crib made of silver and coral, with some gilded brass and ivory, at Compton Verney House in Warwickshire. On a smaller scale, the Victoria and Albert Museum holds a crib made entirely of wax by Gaetano Giulio Zumbo, who is probably better known for his anatomical sculptures.

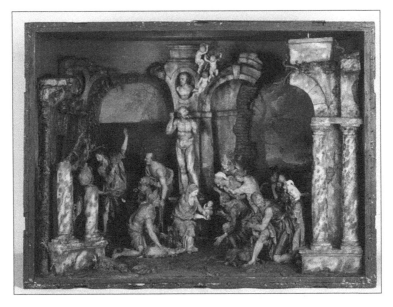

Fig 43: Nativity in wax *by Gaetano Giulio Zumbo (1656–1701) from Sicily, dating to the late 17ᵗʰ century,* © *Victoria and Albert Museum, London*

These cribs do not have moveable figures and are really elaborate ornaments to show off the owners' wealth, perhaps to use as a centrepiece on the dining table at Christmas.

The cribs of Naples and Sicily spread quickly up the Italian peninsula. Whilst Maria Maggiore was content with its nativities of Arnolfo di Cambio and Francesco da Pietrasanta, the Church of San Martino dei Monti in Rome installed a Neapolitan style crib in 1648 for the Carmelite friars. Other churches soon followed.

Another church, that of St Mary of the Altar of Heaven in Rome, added Neapolitan figures to an earlier Baby Jesus figure which was in its possession. This late 15ᵗʰ century Bambino was carved by a Franciscan in the Holy Land from olive wood taken from the Garden of Gethsemane.

On his return to Rome he was shipwrecked, but the little Bambino was discovered washed up on a beach and was taken to Rome, where many miracles were attributed to the statue. The statue was stolen in 1996 and, although it was recovered, it is now kept locked up, and a replica, also carved from olive wood from Gethsemane, takes its place in the crib. Though this church was and is a Franciscan foundation, it was the Jesuits who now led the surge in crib building and the use of Nativity plays to encourage the faith, both in Italy and beyond.

Fig 44: Holy Child of Aracoeli in the Basilica of St Mary of the Altar of Heaven, modern copy of a 15th century original

Spain and Portugal

Naples was ruled by Spain throughout most of the 16th, 17th and 18th centuries, so it is no surprise that Spain also adopted Neapolitan crib types. In addition, however, the 17th century saw the blossoming of Spanish polychromy: sculptures made of a mixture of wood, plaster and terracotta and painted with the utmost realism. Pedro Roldan (1624–1699), a leading sculptor in Spanish polychromy, also sculpted Nativity figures, as did his daughter Luisa (1652–1706), known as La Roldana. Luisa made many smaller Nativity scenes from terracotta, for use in private houses.

A crib by her in the Convent of St Teresa in Madrid has a very tender scene of Our Lady cradling Baby Jesus in her arms. The ox and ass, Joseph, and two shepherds are present and at the back left of the scene is a statue of the donor, the first time this has been seen in a Nativity. The well-known playwright, Lope de Vega (1562–1635), is known to have had his own Nativity sculpted in wax.

In Portugal, Dominican nuns built a Nativity scene in their Lisbon convent in the early 17th century, after one of the nuns had a vision telling her to do so. Whilst similar to Spanish cribs, the Portuguese generally did not go in for all the related genre scenes coming out of Naples. They

Fig 45: Nativity *by Luisa Roldan of polychromed terracotta in the Convent of St Teresa in Madrid*

restricted themselves mainly to the Nativity scene itself and the adoration of the Magi. However, they were not averse to adding in members of the local peasantry as well as the shepherds and, from an early stage, began to add a rooster to the scenes. The rooster was a symbol of good luck in Portugal and announced the birth of Christ by waking the people up for early mass. Midnight mass in Portugal is called Missa de Gallo, Mass of the Rooster. Catherine of Braganza, a Portuguese princess, married Charles II of England in 1662, and was allowed her own Roman Catholic masses in her own Catholic chapel. In 1667, Samuel Pepys went to the Christmas Eve service there, hoping to see a manger with a dressed-up statue of Baby Jesus as a mini-Nativity scene. He was disappointed, but it shows that bringing the statue of Jesus to the altar, and having the crib placed there at Christmas Eve was generally done in Catholic services at Christmas.

France

The small crib did not reach France until the very end of the 17th century. Before then, we have few survivals and they are of the larger kind found in churches. They are also seriously devotional with none of the sense of play

Fig 46: Nativity scenes in St John the Baptist Church, Chaource, Aube, France. Gilded wood, 16ᵗʰ century

or frivolity which had permeated the Neapolitan cribs. The crib at St John the Baptist Church at Chaource in Aube actually consists of two separate scenes and originally had many more figures. It is 16ᵗʰ century, and made of painted and gilded wood. One scene is the Nativity itself which includes Joseph holding St Bridget's candle, and the by now ubiquitous shepherd playing the bagpipes. The other scene has Mary again, this time presenting Jesus to the Magi. Behind are some of their train, including two rather small horses and a very long necked camel.

Fig 47: Nativity at Nogent-le-Rotrou, France, with King David and angels, early 17ᵗʰ century

There is an early 17ᵗʰ century crib at Nogent-le-Rotrou, also made of painted and gilded wood, which includes a statue of King David (Jesus was descended from the line of David), looking very much like King Henry IV of France. The shepherds are dressed in contemporary attire as at Chaource. Our Lady is kneeling devotedly whilst an angel holds up a rather chunky Baby Jesus for us to admire. Towards the end of the 17ᵗʰ century, especially in Provence, the jointed figure from Naples began to appear, as did smaller crib figures made of clay for the ordinary household. We will return to Provence in the next chapter.

Germany, Austria and Bohemia

The lands north of the Alps developed the crib independently from the style of Naples, although wire-framed clothed figures did make their

Fig 48: Maria Anna of Bavaria,
1551–1608. Portrait of 1577
by Cornelis Vemeyen

appearance here too. Some of our earliest evidence comes from the wonderful correspondence between Maria Anna, a Bavarian princess living in Graz, Austria, and her brother, Duke William V, in Munich. In 1577 she wrote to him thanking him for St Joseph, Three Kings, four shepherds, a servant, eight angels and an Old Simeon, which he had sent her for her crib (Krippe). Old Simeon was not present at Jesus' birth but was at the Presentation of Baby Jesus in the temple at Jerusalem for his circumcision, which tells us that Maria Anna was probably arranging various different scenes for her crib. In 1579 she wrote again to ask for Jesus, a Virgin Mary and twelve apostles, which must be made of jointed wire so as to be able to stand, sit or kneel. Although these figures were perhaps for a Holy Week scene (sometimes called a Passion Crib) rather than a Christmas crib, it shows that poseable figures were in use. Maria Anna mentions that they should have 'stuff clothes' and also that she prefers them to those carved and painted figures which are 'horribly expensive'.

Despite the expense, she did buy a carved and painted ox and ass because in one of her letters she says 'little Anna' means to complain to her uncle that she is not allowed to keep the ox and ass for her very own, so her mother suggests that another pair should be sent but that 'if you really want to give them to her let them be large and very strong for they will have to stand a lot of hard wear'! 'Little Anna' was Maria Anna's first child (she managed fifteen children in nineteen years of marriage), Anne of Austria (1573–1598) and was aged four at this time. She later became Queen of Poland-Lithuania and Sweden. This is an early reference linking cribs with children and showing that they could be used as a toy, hopefully an educational one, for children as well as an object of devotion for adults. In 1594 Duke William sent another crib to his three younger brothers who were studying at Ingolstadt, along with a carpenter to erect it for them.

Other record entries show that cribs were becoming immensely popular in private houses as well as churches. This was almost entirely due to the Jesuits, who saw the crib as a valuable tool in encouraging people to meditate on the Nativity. Indeed, in 1619 we have the first description of what a crib is for, by a Jesuit, Philippe de Berlaymont:

'It is common knowledge that the Jesuits are observing the pious custom of their predecessors in the Order, by arranging Christmas cribs to represent the stable in Bethlehem. The manger with the Infant is standing between the Virgin and Joseph in a structure with a roof of straw to which the star is affixed. Shepherds and angels are in attendance, the whole being so cleverly arranged that the devotion of the beholders is vigorously stimulated. They feel themselves to be participating in this so miraculous event, hearing with their own ears the crying of the Child and the heavenly music, touching with their own hands the swaddling clothes, and experiencing a pious awe.'

The Jesuits erected a crib in their church at Prague in 1562 for the Christmas season. In 1582 they built a new church, Holy Saviour, and built a new crib to go in it. In 1601 they erected a crib in a cave scene in Altötting. In 1607 a crib was set up in St Michael's in Munich with cloth dressed figures, and in 1608 they put up a crib in Innsbruck, which inspired the Franciscans to do the same in their church. In Salzburg, the Franciscans, Capuchins and Augustinians all set up cribs in their churches and it is here that we hear for the first time about changing the scenes over the Christmas period. Firstly, a scene of the Annunciation is set up, then the Visitation, Nativity, Adoration of the Magi and finally the Flight into Egypt.

Fig 49: Mechanical crib by Hans Schlottheim made 1585–1588, originally in Dresden Museum

Germans, with their genius for toy making, also developed the first mechanical cribs, although these were undoubtedly toys for adults rather than children and would have fitted into the 'look but don't touch' category. In 1543 Hans Brabender made a clockwork crib for Munster Cathedral. It played 'In Dulci Jubilo' while the Three Kings passed in front of the crib, each bowing in turn.

One of the best of these automaton cribs was made by Hans Schlottheim in the 1580s, for Sophie of Brandenburg to give as a present to her husband, Elector Christian I of Saxony. The main section was gilded brass while the lower tier had a clock and biblical scenes engraved on silver gilt plaques. There were statuettes of the apostles, and also a scene with a Roman soldier holding a child by the hair, and a weeping woman, recalling the Massacre of the Innocents. The second tier was roofed and that had a globe above decorated with the signs of the zodiac. When the clock was wound up, the globe opened to reveal a statue of God the Father surrounded by angels. Then the door in the second tier opened, revealing the Nativity scene. The angels descended from Heaven above to the sound of music, while Joseph rocked the cradle. The ox and the ass knelt down, and then the shepherds and the kings passed by. Sadly, this wonderful crib was destroyed by the allied bombing of Dresden in the Second World War.

Mainly due to the Jesuits, crib building flourished in Germany in the 17th century, and the opening of the crib was often accompanied by the performance of a Nativity play. The archives of Tolz in Mindenheim mention that the boys of the town got so excited by the crib, and caused such a ruckus, that the girls could not continue with their singing practice. In the end the sacristan had to whip the boys out of the church! Convents followed the example of the churches, and the nuns were especially devoted to dressing the figures themselves. However, in some churches the cribs were specialist constructions by artists in many different fields, with endowments to pay for costs and upkeep (and lighting).

We are most fortunate that everything concerning the crib and its accounts was entered in the year 1663 for the crib at Eichstätt Cathedral in Bavaria. Materials listed include silks, ribbons, flowered linen cloth, braid, lace and twenty-four silver buttons. A merchant from Augsburg provided five necklaces of silver beads, and one made of garnets. A lady named as Apollonia Honig was paid for sewing and knitting, including the stockings for the kings, whilst the court tailor was commissioned to make suits, hats, cloaks and arms. Max Caspar Hamel was paid twelve gulden for painting various objects, including animals, jugs and the kings' sceptres. A coppersmith made piping for a working fountain. Other traders employed were a shoemaker, a turner, a glass blower and a cabinet maker. The court furrier made the wigs, and a sculptor in Ingolstadt made all the heads and hands for the figures, as well as the gifts of the kings.

There are further details about the designs of the jewellery, clothes and shoes. The angels had wings made from parrot feathers! One shepherd has red stockings, another has yellow gaiters. One is to pose shielding his eyes from the glory of the angels, another plays the bagpipes, of course. Apart from the ox and ass, there are dogs, goats, stags and eighteen sheep. There is a star above the crib. The crib itself is described as a shed with eaves, typical of the German countryside, and this alone cost 110 gulden. Whilst the figures in this crib were clearly wire figures with carved hands and heads and real clothes, Germany was also well known for figures made of terracotta and especially for those carved in wood and painted. The latter came from the Tyrol, but also from the Black Forest region, and from eastern Germany in the Erzgebirge. Wood figures were made especially for the private home, and often by individuals making them for themselves in the long dark winters. We will come back to those later.

Poland

The Jesuits encouraged the crib when they preached in Poland where wooden 'Bethlehems' or crib altars were already well known. From this tradition, Poland developed its own crib, called a szopka, a large, tiered crib on which a puppet show could be performed. This could also serve as a backdrop for a play, usually performed by boys who would carry the szopka they had made from house to house and perform in front of it. There were also church performances, but these were mostly banned in 1736 by Bishop Teodor Czartoryski when they started to contain contemporary and comic characters rather than sticking to the biblical story. The szopkas later developed into elaborate architectural buildings, a long way from the original Bethlehems, and we will look at these in the next chapter.

Conclusion

The Counter Reformation and the 17th century saw an explosion in the manufacture of cribs. They became ubiquitous in the churches and convents of Catholic Europe, spread especially by the Jesuits, but also by the Franciscans, Augustinians and others. In the later 16th century, the crib also entered private houses as part of the Christmas decorations. In Naples, a whole room might be dedicated to a large crib, whereas in Germany smaller cribs were more usual, placed beneath the Christmas tree when these too came into fashion. Spain and Portugal also had their cribs and, by the end of the 17th century, cribs were being set up in their various overseas territories like the Americas and the Philippines. Germany, especially the Tyrol, established itself as a centre of manufacture and innovation to rival Naples. Evidence for other countries is slight but growing and, in the 18th century we will see the start of the spread of cribs into Protestant north Germany as well.

CHAPTER FIVE

The Crib in the Eighteenth and Nineteenth Centuries

The Apogee and Decline of the Neapolitan Crib

During the 18th century, the crib figure makers of Naples reached extraordinary levels of technical ability. The heads, hands and feet were made from terracotta (or sometimes carved wood) and were hand-painted, often by the same artists working in the new Capo di Monti porcelain factory, which opened in Naples in 1743. The figures' clothes also became more elaborate, often following the fashions of the day with

Fig 50: The Neapolitan royal crib at Caserta Palace, Naples, mid–18th century

extravagances of lace. Our Lady continued to be dressed in light red with a blue cloak, and Joseph in green, purple or yellow. Up to 400 churches in Naples set up a Nativity scene, and there were many cribs in private houses. The owners vied with each other as to who had the grandest crib.

These increasing numbers of cribs, and of the numbers of figures in each crib, saw a reduction in the height of individual figures from nearly 50 cm to around 37–38 cm. Some larger cribs even used smaller figures further back in the scenes to give a sense of perspective. The Dominican preacher, Padre Rocco, encouraged the spread of cribs and had his own made by the poor children of Naples, his own special flock which he looked after. He was greatly admired by King Charles III (1735–1759) and King Ferdinand IV (1759–1825), who encouraged the members of the court to make cribs and crib figures themselves.

Fig 51: The Neapolitan royal crib, detail of the Holy Family

The gentlemen of the court, with help from professional crib makers, would design and make the crib buildings, whilst the ladies of the court cut and sewed, sometimes all year long, in preparation for Christmas. This could be seen as an act of devotion in itself. The clothes were carefully thought out, often copying the fashions of the day. One of the Magi in the Royal Crib wears a mantle exactly copied from that worn by Charles III as Grand Master of the Order of San Gennaro. Although a version of this crib is still displayed at the Caserta Palace near Naples, many of the 18th century figures are now in the Max Schmederer collection in the Bavarian National Museum, Munich. Cribs were, like today, changed from time to time. New figures were brought in, whilst others fell out of favour or fashion. King Charles III was reported to have a figure collection of 5950, so he had plenty to choose from each year! The Schmederer collection also holds a crib constructed by Don Sdanghi, which King Ferdinand offered large sums for, but to no avail.

Although the crib was principally an object of devotion, the Neapolitans also turned it into an enchanting plaything, full of little bits and pieces, which they called 'finimenti'. Inns, which were too full for Mary and Joseph, became full of furniture and fixtures and fittings, as well as customers. There were fruits and vegetables made of wax, crockery made of real china and toys of wood and metal, bone and ivory. The trains of the Three Kings were most elaborate, and the figures here would wear real silver and gold jewellery made by the finest jewellers in Naples. Armour, weapons and horse harnesses were made specially in the royal workshops, and crib artists were sent all over the kingdom to make sure everyone had a chance to buy the best items for their cribs.

Ferdinand IV had a dinner service made at Capo di Monti. He wished to see all the different costumes of his kingdom portrayed on it. Painters were sent to sketch in the most remote hills and mountains, and this scheme also influenced the crib figure makers. Peasant costumes from the Abruzzi region, Calabria and elsewhere became the shepherds of the crib. Real shepherds from Abruzzi would come to Naples in the run up to Christmas and play flutes and bagpipes at all the shrines and cribs set up in the city. Such shepherds, or actors playing the part, can still be seen in the run up to Christmas on the streets of Naples and Rome.

The cribs were often arranged on the top floor or even on the flat roof of the house, so that they might incorporate a real background of trees and mountains, perhaps even Vesuvius. Goethe (1749–1832) travelled in Italy in the Christmas season and describes seeing a rooftop crib in Naples with a great variety of figures and ambitious architecture.

Advent was the time to visit all the cribs and see whose was best. Which ones would the royal family choose to visit this year? The houses of Casa Ruggeri and Casa de Giorgis were known for the best displays. One year, the owner of Casa de Giorgis set out a large separate scene of the torments of Hell! Not very Christmassy, and it caused such a sensation and such large crowds that the following year he replaced it with a more conventional group of the Kings. Signor Rafaello Sorvello hired soldiers to keep the crowds in order at his house. Signor Terres, who ran a bookshop for the rest of the year, turned his premises into a giant crib with many different scenes covering the whole life of Christ. In the Nativity scene, each King had his own large following with a band.

Music played an important part in these crib scenes, both in churches and the aristocratic houses. Scarlatti is probably the best-known composer who wrote compositions both for crib openings and for church services at the crib, but there were many others, such as Christoforo Caresana (1640-1709) who wrote a special composition for the Jesuit church. There were four conservatori in Naples which provided singers and players for these performances. The performances were a great attraction for visitors on the Grand Tour. On one such occasion, Graf Dorne heard a composition by Carmine Giordano called 'Ninna Nanna', composed for the crib in San Domenico Maggiore. He took this back to Vienna and showed it to Beethoven who turned it into his own 'Lullaby'. The song is still played in San Domenico each Christmas.

I have mentioned that many of these cribs consisted of several scenes, generally from the Annunciation through to the Flight into Egypt. The two most popular scenes in Naples, which the crib designers could really get their teeth into, were the scene at the inn and the arrival of the Kings. The Neapolitan inn is full of life and rowdiness. Drunks sing songs and play cards, or dice, whilst minstrels play. The set is full of figures selling their wares of fish, pasta or fruit, whilst the richer clientele step over the beggar by the door. The processions of the kings are grander than any of those real-life ones staged at Epiphany. There are horses, elephants, monkeys, parrots, and marvellous gifts and glittering equipment. Often the kings are depicted as coming from Europe, Africa and Asia, and are mounted on a horse, a camel and an elephant respectively.

An addition at this time was the 'Giorgine', a procession of beautiful ladies from the East, specifically Georgia, bedecked in splendid costumes and jewels. Sometimes a bride is present with her Moorish pages – not really the correct gift for Baby Jesus! All these scenes could spill out into general street scenes of the crowded Neapolitan variety. If you look at a Neapolitan crib you find that Bethlehem has become Naples, and while some of the figures in the crowds are searching for Baby Jesus, others are lost with their own thoughts and lives, and are missing the big event. Neapolitan cribs can be so crowded that we are all perhaps in danger of missing the big event and perhaps that is one idea of these crowded scenes. Just like in our spiritual lives, if you want to find Jesus you really have to look for him.

During the latter part of the 18th century, particular figures started to appear in the cribs, and reasons were given as to why they were there, along with particular items of scenery. These can still be found in many cribs, not just Neapolitan ones, today; They include:-

Benino or Benito: This is a sleeping shepherd in the crib. He is woken by the angels to give him the good news. Children must not wake Benino themselves or the crib of which he dreams will disappear!

The Winemaker and Bacchus: They are here because wine is the gift that Jesus will give us in the Eucharist. Bacchus is the pagan god of wine for whom wine was only a rowdy pleasure. He is a contrasting figure, warning us against the sin of overindulgence.

The Fisherman: These are symbolic of the apostles who were fishermen but were told to become fishers of men. The fish was also the first Christian symbol.

Uncle Vicienzo and Uncle Pascale: These two old men represent the lottery of life, and approaching death.

The Monk: He is often depicted as drunk or fat or indulging in some other sin. The mixture of sacred and profane that is the hallmark of the Neapolitan crib.

The Gypsy: She is a fortune teller and descendant of the figure of the Sibyl in cribs. Often carrying a baby and wearing rich but tattered clothes, a contrasting figure to Our Lady.

Stefania, the mythical mother of St Stephen: Stefania was prevented by angels from visiting Mary at Bethlehem because she was an unmarried woman, so she fooled the angels by wrapping a stone in swaddling clothes and pretending to be a mother. She sneezed when Jesus was born and the stone became a real baby, who would grow up to become St Stephen!

71

Prostitute: Another contrasting figure to the Virgin Mary, she lurks in the vicinity of the inn, far from the Nativity itself.

The Sellers: The various tradesmen and women in the crib came to be sorted by months so that there was a particular tradesperson for every month of the year. For January, there was the butcher, for February the cheese and ricotta seller and for March the chicken seller. Then April was associated with the egg seller, May with a woman selling cherries and June with the baker. In July there was the tomato seller, in August the watermelon seller and in September the farmer. October featured the winemaker, November the chestnut seller, and December the fishmonger.

Other items in the cribs are as follows:

A Bridge: Symbolising the passing from life to death, this world and the next.

An Oven: A reference to bread and the Eucharist.

Church or Crucifix: Obviously anachronistic, this shows us where the Nativity will lead.

The River: Representative of the river of the underworld, the Styx, but also the breaking of Our Lady's waters when Jesus was born.

The Well: The depths of the well lead to the underworld and it was thought bad luck to drink from a well on Christmas night in case one was possessed by a demon. The well is a warning in the Neapolitan crib. Conversely, wells in other cribs may refer to the well where the Angel Gabriel first tried to tell Our Lady about the forthcoming birth of Jesus. Wells might also represent purity and the waters of baptism.

Palm trees: Whilst palm trees could simply show that the events were taking place in the Holy Land (and not in Italy) they can also be seen as a reminder of Jesus' procession into Jerusalem, remembered on Palm Sunday.

The crowds of people in these Neapolitan cribs work so well because many of their designers also worked with the theatre and with organising church parades, where there was a great effort to produce the right effect for the viewers. Many of the crib figure makers and painters were artists in their own right or worked with them. Francesco Celebrano (1729–1814) was also a painter and modeller for Naples porcelain. The Victoria and Albert Museum has a water stoup modelled by him. He was a friend of Padre Rocco and helped make figures for the King's crib. It was Celebrano who first started adding realistic warts and moles to his peasant figures, but he was just as happy with princesses and kings. It was probably Celebrano who first modelled peasants suffering from goitre, a swelling of the neck caused by an enlarged thyroid, a common ailment in Naples at the time. Such figures frequently occur in Neapolitan cribs.

Fig 52: King's attendant by Giuseppe Gori. Metropolitan Museum of Art, New York

Fig 53: Crib figure of a man by Lorenzo Mosca. Metropolitan Museum of Art, New York

Another figure maker was Giuseppe Gori (*fl.*1770–1810) who specialised in fat successful businessmen enjoying the tavern. Illustrated is one of his attendants for the kings which shows the detail and variety of materials that went into these figures. The figure is built on a wire frame wrapped in tow (unspun flax), with limbs of wood and a head of polychromed terracotta. The clothes are made of cotton and satin, with gold and silver metallic thread. The belt is made of velvet backed with leather, the sword is brass, the staff is made of wood and ivory, and there are glass stones set into the turban. The figure is just under 37 cm tall.

Lorenzo Mosca was employed by the Ministry of War, but made crib figures in his spare time, especially studies of country folk. Sometimes he was joined by Tozzi, who was an expert in making hands, full of expression in their own right. There were also those like Nicola and Saverio Vassallo, who specialised in animals. They made terracotta sheep with delicate ears made of metal or wood. Saverio also made horses, and became so popular that he emigrated to Spain to work.

Fig 54: Seated sheep made by Nicola and Saveri Vassallo. Metropolitan Museum of Art, New York

Fig 55: Angel by Giuseppe Sanmartino. Metropolitan Museum of Art, New York

Francesco Gallo modelled more exotic creatures on those he saw in the royal zoo and was even able to model an elephant on one which arrived at Naples with a Turkish embassy!

In the latter half of the 18th century, Giuseppe Sanmartino (1720–1793) emerged as the foremost figure maker. He originally worked in Naples, but later worked also in Florence. He was a leading sculptor of the day, and made the famous figure of the veiled Christ in the Chapel of San Severo in Naples in 1753. Canova said he would give away ten years of his life to possess it. The importance given to crib making is made clear by the fact that this renowned sculptor chose crib figure making as his forte. For him, the figure was more important than the clothes, and his figures have a sculptural quality with exaggerated gestures and expressions which are needed on smaller than life-sized figures. He was the lead artist for the royal crib at Certosa Palace.

Fig 56: King's attendant by Giovanni Battista Polidori. Metropolitan Museum of Art, New York

Followers of Sanmartino included Giovanni Battista Polidori (fl.1781-1802). He was well known as a porcelain sculptor at the Naples factory, but he also made large painted wooden busts for the figures to be paraded in ecclesiastical processions, as well as smaller crib figures.

The detail on this King (Fig 57) by Nicola Ingaldi, another follower of Sanmartino, is superb. The clothes are made from satin, silk and velvet, with gold and silver threads. There are glass buttons, coral beads and small pearls. Finally, the crown is of silver gilt. The King stands 39 cm high on his horse. The Ingaldi family are still in the crib figure making business today.

We have spent a while looking at individual figures by specific artists, and seen the tremendous detail which goes into each one, but Fig 58

Fig 57: Moorish king by Nicola Ingaldi.
Metropolitan Museum of Art, New York

Fig 58: Detail from the Cuciniello crib, Certosa Museum, Naples

shows a glimpse of how these figures appear in a complete crib. Often cited as the finest Neapolitan crib, the Cuciniello crib has around 800 figures in a landscape which is impossible to show in a book – one really needs to see it for oneself. The landscape itself was created by Michele Cuciniello from 1877 to 1879, after he donated his figure collection to the Certosa Museum, but the figures themselves are all 18th century, many by the masters we have been discussing.

Fig 59: Adoration of the Three Wise Men in a Marble Palace,
Bavarian National Museum, Munich

Fig 59 shows a wonderful courtyard scene with the retinues of the kings in a 'crib' constructed by Max Schmederer in *c.*1900. The figures themselves are all 18th century including (in the background) the Holy Family made by Giuseppe Sanmartino, and the Three Wise Men by Lorenzo Mosca, all dating to around 1760. Some of the gifts of the wise men come from the workshops of Sicily. Neapolitan cribs are not all such large panoramas. St Peter's Italian Church in Clerkenwell, London, has a beautiful 18th-century crib with just the Holy Family, Three Kings, one shepherd and three angels. However, it still has everything you would expect to find in a Neapolitan crib: soaring angels in the treetops, a crib set among ruins, a chest of jewels, a censer, little pots and jugs, a bowl of fruit and splendidly dressed figures.

Fig 60: Neapolitan crib in St Peter's Italian Church, Clerkenwell, London

These magnificent cribs could only be afforded by the richest members of society. The poorer people made do with figures carved from wood or moulded from clay or plaster, and either painted or, more usually, simply dressed with whatever material was to hand. There was surely also a trade in second-hand figures and hand-me-downs, as new figures were regularly purchased by the wealthy.

Such an apogee could only be followed by a fall, and the causes were those which occurred elsewhere in Europe, but exacerbated by local factors. There was a general rise in anticlericalism in the later 18th century, as the middle classes and the peasantry thought that the aristocracy and the church were oppressing them, and started to demand more rights and freedoms. In Naples in the 1760s there had been a famine which the King had failed to alleviate adequately. As many as 20,000 people died of starvation in the city itself, and perhaps 200,000 more in the countryside. In 1767, the Jesuits, the great promoters of the crib were expelled from Naples (and Sicily) and their lands partially distributed to poor peasants.

The real death blow, however, came with the French Revolution and the rise of Napoleon. In 1799, King Ferdinand was forced to flee to Sicily when Napoleon instituted a republic, although in the following year the clergy inspired a counter revolution among the peasantry to bring him back, showing that religion was still a strong factor in Naples. However, Napoleon soon came to dominate Europe, and he installed his brother, Jerome, as King of Naples in 1806, followed two years later (when Jerome was made King of Spain) by Marshal Murat. Ferdinand did not regain his throne until 1816. By then, laws passed by both Jerome and Murat had greatly reduced the powers of the church and the aristocracy. Crib making continued, but it no longer had the patronage it had once enjoyed. As Samuel Johnson, the lexicographer, once said, there is nothing that cannot be made a little worse and a little cheaper, and so it was with the Neapolitan crib. Old styles were copied and old moulds were used, and the 19th century offered nothing innovative, only cheaper copies of the glories which had gone before.

Sicilian and Other Italian Cribs

In the 18th and 19th centuries, the crib makers of Sicily continued to flourish, especially at the centres of Caltagirone and Trapani, the latter being especially known for its 'finimenti', those little bits and pieces which give life to a crib, made of precious metals, pearls and coral.

At the top end of the market, entire cribs were still being made at Trapani of coral, silver and ivory for the wealthy, which usually meant for the export market. There was a lovely example by Andrea (1725–1766) and Alberto (1732–1783) Tipa in the Palazzo Torlo Antiques market in Naples recently (Fig 61). Caltagirone, on the other hand, was famous for its pottery figures, the most splendid of which can be seen in the Church of St Mary of Bethlehem in the town of Modica, Sicily. This was made in 1882 by the artists Bongiovanni Vaccaro and Giacomo Azzolina and consists of sixty-two life-size statues made of terra-cotta from Caltagirone. The figures wear typical clothes of the late 19th century except for the Holy Family which, as usual, is depicted in classical style.

Most cribs continued to have carved wooden figures, or occasionally terracotta, with gesso stiffened linen clothes. They could be quite small, less than 30 cm, or larger, up to life-size. Large mechanical cribs were set up at Syracuse and Augusta. Sicilians were even poorer than Neapolitans,

Fig 61: Coral and ivory Trapani crib from the workshop of Andrea and Alberto Tipa, courtesy of the Palazzo Torlo Antiquariato

and this hard life is reflected in the different features of the Sicilian crib. We seldom see the splendour of the kings, and never the vibrancy of the street scene and the inn. What we do get is an interest in the Massacre of the Innocents, a brutal version of which by Giovanni Matera (1653–1718) is in the National Museum of Bavaria. Despite this, the Sicilians also enjoyed depicting the Holy Family as being like themselves and often depicted them in a cosy and playful mood. Mary might take time out to wash clothes and bake bread, while Joseph teaches Jesus the art of carpentry.

Sicily also enjoyed puppet shows of mystery plays, with the jointed puppets made by the same carvers who made the crib figures. As at Naples, shepherds would come down from the hills in the days before Christmas and sing at the various churches. They sang the old story of three shepherds, Bobi, Nencio and Randello, who bring milk and cheese to the crib; of carpenters bringing faggots to light a fire to dry the clothes which Mary has washed, and of the cold being driven away by the warmth of joy brought by Jesus coming into the world. Unlike Naples, Sicily remained under the control of King Ferdinand into the 19th century although it cannot have been completely unaffected by revolutionary events. Nevertheless, its cribs were made by the people for the people and did not rely as much on the aristocratic market as Naples. Sicilian traditions of carved and gessoed linen figures continue today pretty much as they have always done.

In Rome in the 18th century, a tradition began at the Church of St Mary of the Altar of Heaven, where the children of Rome would gather by the Aracoeli statue of Baby Jesus and preach little sermons to passers-by. This tradition still continues today and has been copied elsewhere in Italy. The crib here always displays the Sibyl and the Emperor Augustus, as well as the more usual figures. Early in the 18th century, a Jesuit called Fr Giuseppe de Patrignano wrote a cycle of Nativity plays covering the whole of Jesus' childhood, legends included, for the children of Rome to perform. Here, all the animals of the creation come and kneel at the crib and the birds sing songs and carols.

As for the cribs themselves, they could be quite as elaborate as those of Naples. One Roman prelate became known as the Prelate of the Presepio (Master of the Crib) since he filled his house with figures covering the whole life of Christ, not just the Nativity scenes. Many figures were imported from Naples but others were made locally and, although carved from wood and dressed in real clothes, these usually differ from those of Naples by having heads and hands formed from wax rather than clay, an influence from the Tyrol. As in Naples, cribs were shown to the public, sometimes by appointment, and showings were accompanied by specially composed music. Cardinal Ottoboni commissioned Arcangelo Corelli to write his *Christmas Concerto* in about 1700 for his crib, but there were plenty of other motets and carols that everybody knew and could sing around the crib, whether at church or in their own home. As in Naples, real shepherds would come in from the countryside of the Alban and Sabine Hills, or even from Abruzzi, and sing or play music at the various cribs.

In her 1821 book, *Italy*, Sydney, Lady Morgan (*c.*1780–1859) describes how the shepherds would sing to Our Lady three times a day and would also sing in front of any carpenter's shop they came across 'to honour Mr St Joseph'. Lady Morgan goes on to say that it was the custom to try and visit as many cribs as you could and people who did not were suspected of Jacobinism. Cribs in Rome were (again like Naples) often placed on the top floor of a house to give a real backdrop to the scene through a large window. If such was not available then painted backcloths were used. The crib at the Palazzo Caffarelli-Clementino, now part of the Capitoline Museum, had a backdrop featuring the Tivoli gardens, whilst the crib belonging to Signor Forti, the owner of a glass-making factory, at the top of the Anguillara Tower, had the real landscape immediately behind it for a backdrop.

Fig 62: The Anguillara Tower, on top of which, Signor Forti displayed his crib in the early 19th century

This crib had the scenes carefully arranged to suit the path of the sun so a particular scene would be illuminated at the times of day when Signor Forti's friends came to visit and say their prayers or sing their songs. Few cribs of the period survive today, but it is fair to say that the Roman crib was more often than not arranged in a classical setting of ruined temples, rather than the street scenes of Naples. Romans also liked their mechanisms, and many cribs had a feature called the 'Gloria', where a set of pulleys would lower the angels, and also perhaps, God the Father into the scene. In the 19th century the quality of individual figures declined as they became more numerous but they also became more affordable for all. Cheaper figures began to be made of painted plaster, and these spread to Spain and Marseilles. Joseph Paxton (1803–1865), visiting Rome in 1839 with the Duke of Devonshire (he was his garden designer and would become famous later as the designer of the Crystal Palace), gave us this account of the situation from an Englishman's point of view.

'I saw all their nonsense at Christmas, and longed very much for Blanche (aged 8) and Toey (aged 7) to be here to see the little Jesus which they stick up in most of the churches. In one church they had all the actors complete. First of all there was a model of a stable on a tolerably large scale, in which were placed two small models of oxen lying down quietly, while Our Saviour is represented by a small doll laying quietly in the Manger wrapped up in a little new hay. Close to the Manger stands the Virgin Mother looking very complacently at the little fellow, while Saint Joseph her husband stands opposite looking as if the child before him is a bastard. At a little distance stand the wise men from the east, and at a greater distance are the shepherds in their caves singing "Oh be joyful". Blanche and Toey would laugh at them, while Emily (aged 12) would say, "Oh, Father, what nonsense." Even poor, little George (aged 3) would, I think, laugh at the fun. In some of the churches the figures are made as large as life, but when this is the case there are only three of them, viz., Jesus, Mary and Joseph. The humbug practised on the poor deluded wretches here is horrifying. I have seen in Rome into the inside of one hundred and forty churches.'

This dismissive attitude is typical of the English Protestant distrust of all religious images for most of the 19th century. In the 20th century, however, attitudes changed. Paxton's children may have thought the crib celebrations nonsense and laugh, but his children's descendants would perhaps catch the joy and enchantment which passed him by.

Spain and Portugal

As in Naples, important sculptors of religious statues also made crib figures, and crib making became a recognised craft whose proponents were called *pessebristas*. Several figures made of polychromed terracotta survive from a crib made by José Gines (1768–1823) for King Charles IV of Spain. Life-size figures from a Massacre of the Innocents scene can be seen in the Royal Academy of Fine Arts of San Fernando in Madrid.

There are thirty-four pieces of mothers wrestling with the soldiers who are butchering their children, similar to such scenes in Sicilian cribs and far removed from what we think of as a crib scene today. Other figures by Gines are of various sizes for the same crib, showing that he was using perspective to create scenes in depth. Another great crib maker was Ramon Amadeu (1745–1821) from Olot in Catalonia. Over seventy figures by him are held in the Museu dels Sants d'Olot, where he is seen as the father of the Catalonian crib as opposed to the Spanish, although there is no real difference in styles.

Fig 63: Shepherd playing the bagpipes (1809–1821) by Ramon Amadeu, Museu dels Sants d'Olot

Spanish figures are seldom articulated like those of Naples. The preferred medium is terracotta with occasional wood carvings and then painted. Sometimes real materials are used for costumes in a fusion of styles best exemplified by Francisco Salzillo (1707–1783). He is famous for his great religious statues of scenes from the Passion and he also made large figures for the great religious processions which had grown in pomp since the Counter Reformation. His father had come to Spain from Capua and brought with him Neapolitan crib making traditions. Sadly, much of his work was destroyed in the Spanish Civil War, but the museum at Murcia holds a crib he made for Jesualdo Riquelme between 1776 and 1783, though later figures were added by his students up to 1800. There are 556 figures, each about 30 cm high, made from a variety of materials; terracotta, wood and cloth and set in various scenes from the Annunciation to the Flight into Egypt. The scene of the Nativity itself is unusual in that Jesus is being presented to Mary on a cloth carried by two angels. It looks as if he is a gift from Heaven rather than the result of an actual birth. Murcia remains a centre of crib building in Spain to this day. Spanish cribs became almost as popular as Neapolitan cribs in this period and every region produced their own shepherds and peasants etc in the local costumes. In the 19th century, mass production brought down standards as at Naples, and the turmoil in Spain following the Peninsular War (1807–1814) when Napoleon forcibly placed his brother, Jerome, on the Spanish throne did not help. Later, there was the unfortunate reign of Isabella II (1833–1868) featuring civil wars and revolutions, as well as the expulsion of the Jesuits again in 1820, 1835 and, yet again, in 1868, when Isabella II was forced to abdicate.

Fig 64: Nativity figures by Antonio Ferreira, National Museum of Antique Art, Lisbon

In Portugal, there were two great centres of crib making, Lisbon and Mafra, both making figures in polychromed terracotta. The two most renowned artists were Antonio Ferreira (*fl.*1701–1750) and Machado de Castro (1731–1822). Little is known of the life of Ferreira but his works seems to have been favoured by the Jesuits until their expulsion from Portugal in 1761. Our Lady of Lapa has a Nativity in three scenes: the main Nativity with shepherds, the arrival of the kings, and the Flight into Egypt. His figures of general visitors to the crib give us a good idea of contemporary Portuguese dress. His terracottas were often moulded in large groups and the National Museum of Antique art has many of these on display, though in a sadly damaged state following the 1755 earthquake.

The Bode Museum in Berlin has a well-preserved group of angels showing how these blocks of figures originally looked. Some of these blocks formed part of a vast 500 figure crib made for the Basilica of the Sacred Heart of Jesus in Lisbon, with many different scenes and figures.

*Fig 65: Groups forming the Cavalcade of the Three Kings, Antonio Ferreira,
National Museum of Antique Art, Lisbon*

*Fig 66: Group of angels in terracotta by Antonio Ferreira,
Bode Museum, Berlin*

Machado de Castro, unlike Ferreira, was primarily a sculptor, and is well known for his magnificent equestrian statue of King Joseph I (r.1750–1777). This was erected in the centre of Lisbon in 1775, as part of the rebuilding of the city following the devastating earthquake of 1755. Two cribs of his can be seen in Lisbon. The Basilica da Estrela has a large crib of many scenes and figures made of terracotta, much in the style of a Neapolitan crib. That in the cathedral is more intimate. It has no excess scenes or members of the local populace. The eye is drawn to the simple scene of the Holy Family at the front, while a procession of the kings snakes upwards into the distance.

Fig 67: Crib by Machado de Castro in Lisbon Cathedral, late 18th century

These cribs were for churches and the very rich, but every household could afford a small crib of terracotta figures made by less well known and less skilled artists. Often these cribs, like the large church groups by Ferreira, were made all in one piece like an altar retable. This style of crib proved popular in both the Spanish and Portuguese colonies of South and Central America where the figures were traditionally made by the women of the household. Cribs with separate figures continued to be made through the 19th century. Sometimes they remained the same, sometimes new characters were introduced, but all were of a quite simple style which gradually came to resemble the rustic figures of the 'santons' of Provence and, later, France.

Provence and France

The santons, or 'little saints' that developed in Provence in the later 18th century gradually spread throughout France to become the usual style of French crib. In 18th century France, Neapolitan and Sicilian crib figures were available. They were imported into Marseille and spread from there, but the French were particularly enthralled by their own homemade mechanical cribs. Pope Pius VII often appeared in these cribs after the 1801 concordat he signed with Napoleon, which allowed the Catholic faith to be practised freely again after it was banned during the French Revolution. In one mechanical crib, the Holy Family knelt down for a papal blessing as the pope and his cardinals descended from a carriage. The pope then turned to bless the spectators. In another, Baby Jesus clapped his hands for the pope as he blessed the onlookers, but then hid down in the straw when ships in the harbour fired their cannons! Many cribs had processions of kings and shepherds and attached musical boxes.

By their nature, mechanical cribs tended to be expensive. The French Revolution had swept away the cribs in the churches, and people needed smaller, maybe even secret, crib figures for the home, Ordinary folk needed something cheaper, thus the santon was born. These figures were small, usually about 10 cm high, and made of painted terracotta from simple moulds which could be used again and again. For many decades, it was thought that a mysterious man named Gloriain had made the first of these, as his name appeared on the base of one of a set of 13 cm high 18th century terracotta figures. In the 1950s, a Monsieur Ripert showed that the apparent 'GLORIAIN F' on the figure, thought to stand for 'Gloriain fecit' ('Gloriain made me') was in fact all that remained of a banner description reading 'GLORIA IN EXCELSIS DEO' (Glory to God in the highest) which appears on banners held by angels in many cribs!

The real founder of the santons is now agreed to be Jean-Louis Lagnel (1764–1822), who started to make santons in secret in Marseille from 1797 and openly from 1803, when religious practice was again allowed.

Fig 68: A selection of moulds and santons by Jean-Louis Lagnel,
in the collection of Marcel Carbonel

These little clay figures were air dried and not fired like today's santons, and they were more durable than the painted plaster figures from Naples that were available. After making the main figures of the Holy Family, ox and ass and the Three Kings, Lagnel was inspired by the Neapolitan figures to make models of his friends and neighbours going about their business, or bringing a suitable offering of their own to the manger. Among these figures which can still be seen in the santon cribs of today are The Washerwoman, The Flageolet Player, The Woman with Two Doves, The Spinner, The Man with the Basketwork, The Marmot Trainer, The Vegetable Carrier, The Worshipping Couple, The Baker and The Fisherman. Initially, santons were produced by people part-time while they carried on their normal trades of mason, plasterer or cooper. Inspired by Lagnel, the Batelier brothers started to create santons, along with Antoine Simon. Later, Antoine's son Leon, became one of the leading manufacturers. Production gradually spread from Marseilles to Aix en Provence and Aubagne. By the later 19th century, Toulon had become a major centre with the best figures produced by the Etienne family. From 1803 a fairly regular santon fair took place in Marseille and,

later in the century, some designers introduced new exotic figures such as Turks and Bedouins, along with then current street people like organ grinders with their monkeys.

In the 19th century some larger santons were dressed in real clothes like Neapolitan figures, but the traditional santon is simply painted terracotta, albeit with occasional additions like a real bundle of twigs for a woodsman. The preferred size became smaller over time with figures 5–6 cm high becoming the norm. These cribs never featured the rich aristocracy like Naples – the French Revolution was too fresh in the minds – but they often had a figure of Napoleon to show loyalty to the regime in the early part of the

Fig 69: A group of 19th century clothed terracotta santons, 20 cm high

19th century, and the tradition of having Napoleon at the crib remains in many santon nativities today. Just as the Neapolitan crib became the dominant style on the Italian peninsula, so the Provencal crib became the 'French' crib.

The German Crib

The German crib is that found where German is (or was) spoken: not only Germany, but Austria, Bohemia, Silesia, Switzerland and the Italian Tyrol. In the 18th century the crib flourished throughout these German-speaking lands and despite the worries of the Lutheran clergy, not only amongst the Catholics. Protestant Saxony loved the crib and Goethe saw a crib there in the house of the engraver Stock, placed under the Christmas tree, the latter became a usual location for the crib in the 19th century. As elsewhere, crib making became a recognised art form, and some whole villages became schools of manufacture. Initially these cribs were very similar to Italian ones in style, for that is where the crib tradition spread from.

Fig 70: The crib at Admont Abbey in Steirmark, Austria, by Joseph Stammel,
18th century, carved and painted wood

There in an excellent example of the German baroque crib at Admont Abbey in Austria carved by Joseph Stammel (1695–1765), a sculptor who also carved many statues still preserved in the library there. The figures were painted by Anton Pottschnigg. The crib consists of three tiers, one above the other. The first is a Nativity, with kings to the left and bakers to the right, one carrying a loaf of bread in the shape of the abbey's arms. Above that, a shepherd with his flock of sheep is awoken by an angel and, at the top, is a scene of the Presentation in the Temple. This latter, celebrated by the church on 2nd February as Candlemas, is the traditional date for taking cribs down. At Admont, the crib doors are opened on Christmas Eve and closed on February 2nd. Included in this crib are two birds: an owl, representing the wisdom of the pagan past, about to be overturned by the truth of Christianity; and a parrot representing the pharisees, presumably because it looks lovely and can speak but lacks true understanding. In the temple scene there are three women representing Faith, Hope and Love. So, in a similar way to a Neapolitan crib, this is a large design with scenes and many figures, but here Jesus is plain to see and is definitely the centre of attention.

Figures made of clay feature in the Tyrol and Bavaria but wood carving certainly predominated, and it is this style which spread northwards. In each region, a family crib was made of whatever materials were close at hand. The wealthy could use the service of a professional figure carver and those from the Tyrol were very much in demand outside their area, particularly in Bohemia and the Czech lands beyond. Native Bohemian crib makers then began to flourish in Iglau, Zwittau and Schluckenau. The carvers of Oberammergau, famed for its Passion Play, carved many a crib figure, and Salzburg became another centre. Austrian and Bohemian cribs tended towards the ambitious, and were particularly fond of placing the Nativity scene in a large castle or church setting, based on real buildings throughout the country. Early figures were clay or even cardboard, but under Joseph II (1741–1790), the carved wooden figures of the Italian Tyrol became fashionable, usually with fabric clothing.

Fig 71: Crib from the Servite convent at Innsbruck, now in the Bavarian National Museum, Munich, c.1750

Terracotta was a popular medium in parts of Austria, Westphalia, Swabia and the Black Forest. Here, the figures were small and even the background landscapes were modelled in clay. Augsburg specialised for a while in wax figures. There is a lovely mid-18th-century survivor from the Servite convent at Innsbruck, now in Munich. Here the figures are carved of wood with limbs attached to the torso with wire and the heads moulded in wax. There are shepherds to the left and kings to the right (dressed like Austrian aristocrats) and a long row of sumptuously dressed angels. The bright robes of the Holy Family and their central position make sure that they stand out as the centre of attention. These figures will have been dressed by the nuns themselves as an act of worship, but it is likely that the figures were professionally made.

The china factory in Vienna turned out china cribs, and cribs also appeared made of prints pasted onto cardboard with painted backdrops. The mechanical crib was also popular. In 1770, Aachen had a crib which featured scenes from both the Old and New Testaments in which 'everything moves, stands or speaks'. This was perhaps clockwork though no one today knows quite how the 'speaking' was done! There were also cribs powered by water in much the same way as the many waterworks of 18th-century gardens, like that at the Hellbrunn Palace, Salzburg.

The puppet play based around the crib also flourished, although this was often a secular or topical affair with a crib standing in front of the stage as the excuse for a show. The puppets were made by craftsmen who also made crib figures and is perhaps why the dressed doll became the most popular type of crib figure in southern Germany, especially Bavaria. These figures are often elaborate, like the Servite convent crib in Fig 71, especially the kings and angels. The background too was important, with mountain ranges or local buildings made of wood, cork and cardboard. These became especially central in Bohemia and were also used as backgrounds for plays and songs performed by children.

Fig 72: Pair of angels in polychromed linden wood by Ignaz Günther, 16–17 cm high, c.1753

There was also a different trend towards the homely rather than the courtly, with concentration again on the Holy Family and the shepherds, rather than kings and angels. It was this sort that tended to be made in the home rather than by the professional crib maker, but both sorts happily coexisted. Indeed, Germans embraced the crib in all its many varieties of style and materials. Let us look at some of the more important makers.

Ignaz Günther (1725-1775) was a sculptor based in Munich. He carved stone statues for churches, but also wooden crib figures in a late baroque or rococo style. He is famous for his angels. Franz Xavier Nissl (1731-1804) was expert in portraying the characters of locals he saw, which he then turned into shepherds and other passers-by, although he is perhaps better known for his painting rather than his figures today.

Fig 73: The Flight into Egypt by Johann Schwanthaler at Altmünster, Austria, c.1770

There is a beautiful crib by Johann Georg Schwanthaler (1740–1810) at the parish church of Altmünster in the Salzkammergut region in Austria. This consists of seven scenes including the Presentation in the Temple, the scene where Jesus is found in the temple aged twelve; and the Flight into Egypt. The exotic animals with the Kings are slightly unusual because Schwanthaler had clearly never seen a camel or an elephant. These figures are all of polychromed lime wood. Johann was the son of sculptor and crib figure carver, and later generations of the Schwanthaler family were also involved in figure making, but Johann was the most skilful, and his figures are still copied today in the Salzburg region of Austria.

Fig 74: Jesus in the Temple aged twelve (c.1800) by Johann Giner the Elder. Tyrolean Folk Art Museum

Fig 75: The Brugger Nativity in the Tyrolean Folk Art Museum in Thaur, early 19th century. Figures by Johann Giner the Elder, mountain scenery by Felix Zimmerling (1812–1869), background painted by Johann Leith (1775–1863). Tyrolean Folk Art Museum

Another family whose work developed into a school of crib makers was the Giner Family of Thaur. The founder of the dynasty, Johann Giner the Elder (1756–1833) led the way from the Baroque and Rococo crib into the less formal crib style of German Romanticism. Cribs in the 'Giner style' are still made in the Tyrol today.

Painters like Johann Leith became more involved with crib figures as the 19th century progressed and were in demand for the detailed painting of wax heads and hands as well as crib backcloths. One of the best painters from the 18th century was Christoph Anton Mayr (1720–1771) from Schwaz, nineteen miles east of Innsbruck. He painted many frescoes in churches but also backgrounds for cribs. He was also a leading proponent of painted flat card crib figures, which were developed around the middle of the 18th century.

Fig 76: Nativity scene made of painted card in the Church of St Peter and St Paul, Telfs, west of Innsbruck, painted by Christoph Anton Mayr in 1767

His crib at Telfs had three interchangeable scenes for displaying the Adoration of the Shepherds, the Adoration of the Kings, and the Presentation in the Temple. In his home town of Schwaz, there is an 'all year round' crib of 525 card figures which have scenes of Jesus' life all the way from the Nativity to the Crucifixion and Resurrection. His figures are beginning to show the change from Baroque to the new more relaxed Romantic style. His scenes aften clearly depict a Germanic countryside but with the odd palm tree thrown in so you know you are in the Holy Land.

As with other European countries, the crib had a rough time in Germany during the enlightenment and subsequent bouts of anticlericalism. The Jesuits were officially shut down by the pope in 1773, although their work continued to be allowed in Prussia, and the order was restored in 1814. In 1782 Austria and Hungary closed hundreds of monasteries and banned Capuchins, Carmelites. Carthusians, Cistercians, Dominicans, Franciscans and Poor Clares. Religious orders were forbidden from teaching. Many large cribs were broken up and lost. In 1770, the Holy Roman Emperor Maximilian III Joseph banned all religious plays (except the Passion play at Oberammergau), and they remained banned until 1814. But the anticlericalism was not widespread among the general population and cribs continued to be made, especially in the Tyrol. Indeed, the lack of the great cribs in monasteries and, to an extent, in churches, encouraged the creation of smaller cribs in private houses.

A major influencer of 19th century-crib making in southern Germany was Joseph von Führich (1800–1876) from Bohemia, who was a member of the Nazarene group of German speaking artists who studied in Rome between about 1810 and 1830. The Nazarenes were similar to the Pre-Raphaelite movement in Britain, wishing to get away from Neo-Classicism and create more realistic and romantic art, particularly religious art. Joseph von Führich was much influenced by Dürer, and devoted himself to religious works. He painted many crib scenes, frequently on paper, and developed the homely scene set in the Holy House with carpentry tools lying about. This became a popular scene in Germany due to the many woodworkers who also made cribs. Painted backgrounds were essential, but the Nativity could be set in a stable, and in the rolling hills of Germany, or in a more realistic Palestine. In the 19th century more people were travelling to the Holy Land and writing books with illustrations, so crib makers were able to get a clearer idea of a realistic landscape.

This scene by Max Gehri shows how multitalented these crib makers were. He has carved and painted the figures at the well and clothed them splendidly. In the background are two camels, one of which is a figure, the other part of the painted background, giving a wonderful depth to the scene. Max Gehri (1847–1909) was a follower of the Nazarenes and was a well-known artist and fresco painter before turning to crib making in later life.

Fig 77: Women at a well with camels in the background.
Nativity scene by Max Gehri

Fig 78: Annunciation by Johann Berger, c.1850,
in the Bavarian National Museum

In a similar style, using clothed wooden figures, is the Annunciation by Johann Berger in the Bavarian National Museum, which is part of a Holy House at Nazareth scene. However, he could also dispense with the material and just use carved and painted figures, like this wonderful group of Moors, part of the retinue of one of the kings. Their tunics look like cloth but are actually carved in the wood. Berger worked in Munich and the crib carving business is continued today by the fifth generation.

Fig 79: Group of Moors by Johann Berger, before 1850,
in the Bavarian National Museum

Another Munich artist was Anselm Sickinger (1807–1873) who started life as a stone carver but soon turned to wood. Like Berger and Gehri, he preferred the clothed crib figure, but his carved figures tended to be jointed on a wire frame, with carved heads and hands, rather than a solid carved figure.

The crib setting, although relatively modern, is of a style well known in the 19ᵗʰ century – an old wooden building in an alpine setting, complete with snow. Similar figures were made by the Lang family of Oberammergau and are still made today by the firm of Richard Lang. A colleague of Sickinger for a while was Josef Knabl (1819–1881), who was born at Fliess in the Tyrol. He studied woodcarving at Munich and made the 'Coronation of Our Lady' in the Munich Frauenkirche. Woodcarving in the Italian Tyrol centred round the town of Bosen/Bolzano, and although some carvers travelled to Munich to study, or to the south in Italy, many were content to stay put and hone their skills at home. Today there is a flourishing Bolzano woodcarving industry, including cribs, and there is a trademark to ensure high standards are kept.

Fig 80: Crib figures by Anselm Sickinger in the Bavarian National Museum, c.1840. The stable dates from 1959

Fig 81: Carved wooden crib from Oberammergau in the Bavarian National Museum, 19th century

Oberammergau also remained and continues to grow as a centre of woodcarving. The Bavarian National Museum has a particularly beautiful example carved in linden wood in the gothic style but left unpainted, artist unknown (Fig 81).

Fig 82: Paper cut out crib figures designed by Joseph Bachlecher, c.1900

Joseph Bachlecher (1871–1923) was born in the Tyrol and was one of those who went to study in both Munich and Rome. His main work dates to the early 20th century when he was commissioned to carve many altarpieces and statues for churches, but he specialised in cribs and also designed lots of paper cut out crib figures whose designs are still being used today.

Fig 83: Crib made with paper cut out figures by Wenzel Fieger
in the Bavarian National Museum, c.1890

Crib figures made of paper or card boomed in the later 19th century because, once the initial design was there, they could be printed cheaply for families to colour in at home. Wenzel Fieger (1860–1924) showed that a paper crib could also be an impressive crib, as evidenced by his Nativity of several hundred figures, now in the Bavarian National Museum. Wenzel came from Moravia, and paper cribs were especially popular there and in neighbouring Bohemia. There is an excellent collection of paper cribs at the Stadtmuseum of Steyr, near Linz, in Austria.

Elsewhere in Europe

Warsaw and Krakow continued to develop the Polish crib, the *szopka*, in the later 18th and 19th centuries. The large wooden and cardboard scenes of Warsaw tended towards imaginary architecture, whilst those of Krakow often copied existing buildings, usually churches, in the city. The Nativity figures tended to be carved of wood and dressed in material clothes and could also be puppets used for a puppet play. The szopkas could be carried door to door as part of a carolling service, but these were suppressed by the occupying Germans and Austrians in the First World War, more as an anti-Polish drive rather than anti-crib. Door to door carolling with a crib was also prevalent in Hungary and Czechoslovakia, whilst another idea was for nine families to come together for the Novena of Christmas (the nine days leading up to Christmas). One crib would be shared between the nine, each family having it for one day of the novena.

The crib had possibly appeared in England before the Reformation but there is no evidence for it. The early Anglican church was Protestant enough to be wary of anything that reminded them of the Catholic faith. They would call cribs 'popery', especially after the trials of the Civil War and the reign of the inept catholic king, James II (1685–1688). A possible early mention of a crib in England comes from a description by A J Kempe of Christmases celebrated by Queen Charlotte (who was from Mecklenburg-Strelitz in north Germany) at Windsor Castle in the 1780s and 1790s. A member of her household set up a Christmas tree for a children's party, beneath which was 'a neat model of a farmhouse surrounded by figures of animals'. This sounds suspiciously like a crib but with the Holy Family removed, in case of offence, perhaps?

The anti-Catholic and therefore anti-crib ideas persisted into the 19th century when the Oxford Movement, led by Edward Pusey and

Cardinal Newman, reintroduced various old Catholic traditions to the Anglican church. At about the same time, in the 1840s, other Christmas 'traditions' began, such as the Christmas tree in private houses, crackers, the Christmas card, the advent calendar etc, so it was easy for the crib to become a tradition too. Since then, Nativity scenes have appeared in many Anglican churches and still do today. There had been some remaining Catholics in England since the Reformation, but they did not have full rights as citizens until 1829. In 1850 Catholic bishops were allowed and the Catholic church was fully restored in Britain. This was probably an influence on the Oxford Movement. The Catholics had cribs of course, but there were as yet no native craftsmen. The cribs were brought in from Italy and Germany. Even in Ireland, where the majority population was Catholic, there is very little evidence for cribs before the 18th century. One feels some churches must have had them, perhaps locally made, while richer churches could import them from Italy and Germany.

Outside Europe

As mentioned previously, it was the Jesuits who helped to spread the crib around the world through their missionary work. In the 1590s, cribs had been set up at colleges in Indo-China, Japan, Goa and Lahore. In the 17th century, cribs were introduced to the native Americans where a French Jesuit, Saint Jean de Brébeuf wrote the first Christmas carol in a native American language, Huron. These cribs were all of European type, imported with the missionaries. In the 18th century local makers in both north and south America created their own 'santos', or 'little saints', usually in terracotta. These died out a century later with the coming of railways and cheap ready-made cribs, but there has been a revival since the 1950s. A similar story can be seen in Africa, although it is not until the very end of the 19th century at the earliest, that locals start making their own cribs set in African villages with a black Baby Jesus.

CHAPTER SIX

The Modern Crib

It is true to say that during the 20th century, and into the 21st, the crib has spread worldwide and there are many books, such as that by James Govan (see the bibliography) which illustrate many cribs in many different styles from many different countries. For this modern period, unlike in previous chapters, it is impossible to cover all important artists and trends, but I will try to cover all the main aspects of cribs and crib building, that seem important or interesting and apologise now if your favourite artist or crib style is not here. The reasons for the proliferation of the crib are manifold. Missionary activity during earlier centuries has led to the spread of Christianity around the world, and many different cultures now want a crib that represents their own traditions. More importance is attached to childhood as a special phase of development and the idea that children should not simply be treated as mini adults. More children's books and toys are made especially for them. More cribs are now made as toys. Finally, there is the growth of leisure time, which has led to an increase in the appreciation of the art of the crib and in the desire to make cribs oneself as a leisure activity.

Friends of the Crib

Artisans concerned with the construction of cribs and crib figures often came together in informal associations to learn from one another and to promote their work to patrons. The Nazarenes of Germany were one such group and a Crib Association was formed by makers in Barcelona in 1863. The nature of these groups changed during the First World War (1914–1918). Whilst the dreadful times turned many people away from God, many people also turned towards God as their only salvation. Groups gathered to promote the idea that every home should have a crib, and to help each other to preserve crib (and other Christmas) traditions, as well as exploring new crib designs. A group formed in Salzburg in 1916, and perhaps some years earlier among the woodcarvers of South Tyrol. Another group started in Munich in 1917, but the real flourishing was 1919, when the war ended and Christianity had to contend with communism. Friends of the Crib groups were founded in this year in Bamberg, Altötting, Augsburg and many other German cities and towns. In the USA, the Jesuit Paul Sauer founded a group in 1920, though this was short-lived. The idea spread throughout Catholic Europe and South America and, after the Second World War (1939–1945), these groups came together to form national bodies. Italy's Association was founded in 1953, Austria's in 1954, Spain's at Madrid in 1944 while the Spanish Basques established their own in 1947.

In 1952 the World Federation of Friends of Cribs was founded as an umbrella organisation. Its Latin name, the Universalis Foederatio Praesepistica is generally known by the abbreviation Un-Foe-Prae. Its remit is to further knowledge of the crib's history and to promote the crib as an aid to devotion. It is also to encourage members to help each other in the construction and display of cribs, to which end they have established conventions and exhibitions around the world. The Federation has had some ups and downs. In 1952 groups from Bolivia and Chile were present although they no longer exist today. The American Christmas Crib Society, founded after the Second World War by the Reverend Aloysius Horn, folded in 1971 following his death, and Un-Foe-Prae had its divisions in the 1960s between conservatives and liberals.

The accession of John Paul II in 1978, the first non-Italian pope for centuries, gave a boost to the Catholic church and to national Friends of the Cribs Societies, which joined the international body: France in 1978, South Tyrol (1979), Switzerland (1983), Liechtenstein (1984), Malta (1986), Belgium (1991), Czech Republic (1994), the Belgian Flemish Society (1995), USA (2000), Slovenia (2001) and Colombia in 2005. Beneath these national societies are many smaller groups. Nearly every town in Spain, Germany and Italy will have a Friends of the Crib group. For example, the Catalonian group in Un-Foe-Prae represents over sixty small town groups. These societies have different emphases. Some keep museums of old cribs, others have competitions for cribs and put on shows at Christmas. Nearly all have workshops and craftsmen only too willing to help beginners with their first crib or their 101st! The Christmas crib will continue to thrive under their management.

Germany, Austria, Switzerland and the Tyrol

Fig 84: Crib at St Martin's Church, Allgäu, 1920 by Sebastian Osterrieder

A leading crib builder in Germany in the early 20th century was Sebastian Osterrieder from Bavaria (1864–1932). He was carving crib figures from lime wood by 1900 and in 1910 he travelled to Palestine and Egypt for inspiration and accuracy in designing the buildings and landscapes. In 1913 he carved forty figures for the crib at the Neuer Dom in Linz, Austria. His crib at St Martin's Church, Allgäu, shows the arrival of the shepherds who are carefully dressed as Palestinian shepherds of the time. His great innovation was to be able to cast further copies of his work as reinforced plaster casts on a wire frame, known as reinforced or hard casts. Thus these figures could be carved once but then be purchased by many other churches or households who wanted them.

Many other Bavarian woodcarvers adopted the hard casting technique, which helped make quality figures more widespread. Otto Zehentbauer

Fig 85: The Three Kings by Otto Zehentbauer in the Bavarian National
Museum, 1924–1925

(1880–1961) was a leading light in the Bavarian Crib Friends and a
religious statue sculptor of note. He carved wooden figures and used the
hard casting technique as well as making figures with wire-framed bodies,
wood carved heads, and dressed in material. His figures, and most others
between the wars, stuck to fairly traditional Romantic/Neo-Gothic lines,
but more modernist ideas were penetrating the wood carving school at
Bad Warmbrunn in Silesia.

Fig 86: Crib by Wilhelm Kunst, painted wood, 1930s

In this crib (Fig 86) by Wilhelm Kunst (1909–1986), the figures have a much simpler line. Kunst was born near Oldenburg in Lower Saxony and studied at the Bad Warmbrunn school in the 1930s. The school flourished until 1945, when Silesia became Polish. The school of woodcarving was closed and the German population expelled. Bad Warmbrunn is now known as Ciepliece. But though the Silesian school may have closed, its tradition of woodcarving survived in homes in other parts of Germany. The Black Forest region and Oberammergau remain as centres of woodcarving, sometimes painted, as does the Erzgebirge. This region, bordering the Czech Republic, was an important mining area from the 16th century, but in the dark winters or on the occasions when the mines were not working, the men turned to woodcarving and found a ready market in nearby Dresden. The style of figures developed into a recognisable regional design with simple, almost peg-like figures, beautifully painted and only about 8–9 cm high.

Fig 87: Erzgebirge crib, c.2000, by Gudrun Galler for Käthe Wohlfahrt

Fig 87 shows a modern Erzgebirge style crib by Gudrun Galler (1949–2020), which was sold as a limited edition through the Käthe Wohlfahrt Christmas shops. This shop began in Rothenburg ob der Tauber in Bavaria, so it interesting that they chose to go with an Erzgebirge style crib from East Germany. The figures are made from many separate pieces of wood, glued together and then hand painted by Gudrun. Apart from the main crib shown here, many other figures and buildings as well as a background painted landscape were produced. The crib was also fitted with electric lights, a post war innovation to the Nativity scene.

Another Erzgebirge speciality is the 'Pyramide' (Pyramid). In the 18th century, the carvers were making wooden stands with candles on to light their homes and they began to add figures to these. In the 19th century, the all-round stand shaped like a Christmas tree was made to be lit up at Christmas and, some time later, these 'Pyramiden' were built around a central spindle with a propellor at the top. The heat from the candles spins the propellor and the figures march around in a circle. Many different figures can be placed on a Pyramide, but it is likely that Nativity scenes were the first and they remain the most popular. That shown in Fig 88 has a static Holy Family in the centre, around which the shepherds march. The

Fig 88: 'Pyramide' crib from the Erzgebirge, 1990s, by Richard Glässer of Seiffen

upper tier has an angel appearing to shepherds while more angels blow trumpets at the top. The bottom tier has a revolving procession of the Three Kings and their camel handler. This 'Pyramide' was made by Richard Glässer whose firm was founded in Seiffen in the Erzgebirge in 1932.

Fig 89 shows a different form of Erzgebirge carving by Uwe Uhlig who specialises in miniatures. This scene shows the Three Kings riding an elephant, a horse and a camel and is not much bigger than a matchbox on its side, the elephant rider is only 2.5 cm high. Uwe has also carved a matching Nativity scene in the stable, and a scene featuring the angel appearing to the shepherds. The Three Kings scene was bought at Cologne, where the cathedral has a shrine to the Three Kings. These scenes are the only religious scenes Uhlig has made, a development which occurs more and more in the later 20th century. Craftspeople who are specialists in other fields such as china, glassware, knitting, now all tend to have a go at making a Nativity scene.

Fig 89: The Three Kings by Uwe Uhlig of Lengefeld in the Erzgebirge, c.2000

The artists of the Erzgebirge, like those of South Tyrol, have a guild to which members who achieve the highest standard of woodcarving belong. They can then mark their wares with a special label. This is important. Many cribs made today in what looks like an Erzgebirge style are in fact of lower quality manufactured in China, where they have been made since the 1980s.

Fig 90: Annunciation using Huggler figures, from Brienz, Switzerland, c.2010

Fig 91: Nativity Scene using Huggler figures, c.2010

The figures in Figs 90 and 91 are made by Huggler of Switzerland, a crib specialist. Hans Huggler-Wyss designed these 'flat cut' carved wooden figures in 1915. They are still made today by the firm he founded in Brienz. Hand-painted as well as carved, these figures are 14 cm high, although the firm now does other ranges, varying from 12 cm up to 63 cm, figures big enough for a church. The joy of a crib with separate figures is that as advent advances, you can begin with an Annunciation scene and use the same figures again later for a Nativity scene. Huggler went on to become a leading art deco wood carver in the 1920s, but his 1915 crib remains his crowning glory.

Ostheimer, from Baden-Württemberg, are responsible for another classic German crib design. The firm began in the late 1930s making wooden toys but, went bust in 1950 because of the huge influx of plastic toys from the USA. It re-founded itself in 1958 employing disabled people to make simple wooden toys. From this new beginning, came a design for simple wooden crib figures made especially as toys for children. The firm has flourished in recent decades with the desire of many parents to stop using plastic, as well as a sense of nostalgia for old wooden toys. The figures are both stylish and robust.

Fig 92: Annunciation scene with Ostheimer figures, Göppingen, Baden–Württemberg, 1990s

Fig 93: Joseph leading a pregnant Mary to Bethlehem on the donkey. Ostheimer figures, 1990s.

Fig 94: The Threes Kings have an audience with King Herod and his crow. Ostheimer figures, 1990s

Fig 95: The Nativity with angels and shepherds. Ostheimer figures, 1990s.

As with the Huggler figures, the Ostheimer figures can be arranged in different scenes. In our own home we normally have the Annunciation in the first week of advent, then Mary on her donkey in week two. In week three we set up the crib with the shepherds whilst the Three Kings talk to Herod. (Apart from Ostheimer, Fontanini of Italy does a Herod figure and there must be others.) At Epiphany, the Three Kings join in the main crib scene and even Herod's crow turns up at the crib. Herod does not go to the crib but is left alone in a dark corner! Some crib makers, including Huggler and Ostheimer, make a figure of Mary on a donkey carrying Baby Jesus, which can be used for a Flight into Egypt scene.

Further south in the Austrian Tyrol, the Anri workshop, founded in 1937 in St Ulrich, produces traditional carved wooden cribs and crib figures as does the family of Albert Comploj at Ortisei in the Italian Tyrol. His figures are carved from maple or lime wood and can be painted. They come in sizes from 9 cm to 115 cm. Ortisei is also the home of Bernardi, who make figures in a variety of styles; traditional, baroque, modern, and figures specially for children similar to the Ostheimer pieces. Bernardi was founded in 1960.

Also at Ortisei, Leo Prinoth founded the firm of Lepi which has been woodcarving since 1920. Their main collection of Nativity figures is in the baroque style, more Italian than German. They were designed by Prugger Dorigo Vigil (born 1925) and are hand-painted. Lepi also however do a series of clothed figures on a wire frame, a style especially popular in Bavaria. Altogether in the Val Gardena in South Tyrol, there are over forty different woodcarving studios, so I have only scratched the surface here. They display their wares every Christmas at a market in Santa Cristina.

Fig 96: Our Lady and a page by Lepi, 2020, carved wood in the baroque style, South Tyrol

Fig 97: The Holy Family by Lang, 2020, Oberammergau, clothed figures on a wire frame, wooden heads and hands

At Oberammergau in Bavaria, the firm of Lang has been making figures since 1775. These days their figures have a plastic torso supporting the wire frame, with heads, hands and feet carved from wood and then dressed. The figures can be posed to stand, sit or kneel, and come in various sizes from 16 cm to 40 cm. The figures also come in two different styles, Oriental (i.e. 1st century AD, authentic) and Bavarian (19th century clothes). At the Christmas Market in Munich there is a separate market called the Krippenmarkt which is simply for cribs and crib figures and accessories. Apart from carved wooden figures, many sell wire figures with wooden heads and hands so that the home crafter (often a member of a local Friends of the Crib group) can dress the figures themselves.

Making homemade cribs and crib figures has become much more popular since the start of the 20th century. As to the accessories, one is reminded of the Neapolitan 'finimenti'. Small pots, straw bales, buckets and agricultural tools are just some of things available to decorate the crib scene. There is also equipment for lighting up the scene with electrics. Miniature lanterns can be plugged in, but also realistic looking camp fires and even water effect fountains. The more ambitious crafter can turn a crib almost into an automaton with moving figures.

The 20th century has seen the great expansion of the Christmas market, especially in Germany or in a German style. There is a German Christmas Market in Birmingham each year, as well as in many other English towns. These will all have a Nativity scene, if not a whole collection of them. If it snows enough, then Munich will build a crib out of snow, and many fairs have giant revolving 'Pyramiden' with life-size crib figures within. Another feature of German towns at Christmas time is the 'Krippenweg', or Way of the Crib. Many shops will have cribs of different designs in their windows, and a leaflet is produced listing these so that you can tick off as many as possible around the town. Some crib societies actively encourage this, and will lend cribs out to shops who haven't got the time or inclination to set up their own.

Nativity sets began to be made from other materials in the 20th century in Germany. Nuremberg was the centre of toy manufacture, especially tin plate toys and lead soldiers, from the 19th century. The favoured style of toy soldiers was 2.8 cm tall flat cast figures or 'flatties', which are shallow cast so as to be virtually two-dimensional, unlike the larger hollow cast three dimensional figures like the UK's well-known Britains toy soldier figures.

Fig 98: Miniature Nativity made in tin, c.2000, from Nuremberg, Germany

Fig 99: Shepherd made from Elastolin by Hausser, 1925

Apart from soldiers, nativities could also be made, and these were particularly popular from *c.*1900 through to the 1930s, when three-dimensional figures made of Elastolin, a mixture of glue and sawdust, began to supplant them. Today, tin flat figures are popular again, especially in miniature versions. That shown in fig. 98 fits into a matchbox.

The Elastolin mixture was invented by the firm of Hausser at the beginning of the 20th century and was used until 1969. Plastic was introduced in 1955, and gradually replaced Elastolin. From the beginning, Hausser manufactured crib figures as well as the more usual soldiers. They could be bought painted or plain. The firm was taken over by Preisser in 1983. Preisser is particularly well known for its model railway accessories, but also makes Nativity figures, in plastic, in many different sizes in a traditional style. The firm of Schleich, better known for its toy animals and fairytale figures, also brought out a plastic crib in a more baroque style to celebrate the millennium in 2000. Plastic has become the usual material now these for small cheap crib figures that can be found in many households but they are often very well made and hard to tell from carved wood or plaster pieces unless handled.

Fig 100: Playmobil Nativity set, early 21ˢᵗ century, Germany

One crib that is obviously plastic is that made by Playmobil, the maker of children's toys. Playmobil figures were first made in 1974 by the Brandstätter Group, based at Zirndorf near Nuremberg. These 7.5 cm figures became popular very quickly and are now a world bestseller. They have made at least half a dozen different cribs over the years. These are clearly made as playthings for children, but there are also adult Playmobil collectors and the figures are very authentically designed for first century Palestine. One of Playmobil's main competitors is Lego from Denmark. Both firms often have similar themes in their toys and it is surprising that Lego have never made a crib set, although various amateur brick builders have of course made their own nativities from available Lego pieces.

Italy

In Italy, the main centre of quality crib production switched from Naples to South Tyrol which I covered in the previous section. In Naples, there was still a reliance on plaster casts of old figures by Sanmartino,

Celebrano and others. While quality fell, it did mean that every house could have a crib. New and better sculptors in plaster started to appear throughout Italy towards the end of the 19th century. Monaco Museum has a crib by Gia Sanmartino with whole figures sculpted in plaster and painted. Figure size also reduced to 15–20 cm, which allowed for larger more realistic scenes. Clay sheets could be added to the figures to create cloaks etc. These little figures were known as 'petobelle' after 'pettola', a Neapolitan word for a pasta sheet.

The 1931 play, *Christmas in the Cupiello House* is based around the main character's need to set out the crib for Christmas and shows the central part the crib played in a Neapolitan household. While Umberto Grillo (see bibliography) sees the Italian family today as just as likely to be gathered around the Christmas tree or the television set, the fact that *Christmas in the Cupiello House* was made into a successful film in 1977, and again as recently as 2002, shows the crib can still have its place at the centre of the house at Christmas.

Fig 101: Italian (mostly) crib figures from the 1940s and 1950s in plaster and plastic

Italian plaster figures were widely exported and are the source of many late 19th century and early 20th-century cribs in Britain, both for churches and the private house. Fig 101 shows my family crib, bought in stages after the Second World War. Mary, Joseph and the donkey were bought in Woolworths in Wimbledon 1946. The kings followed in the 1950s, by which time the plaster figures were no longer being made. Despite being a perfect match for the Holy Family and probably made by the same (unknown) firm, the kings are made of lightweight plastic. The ox met an early death in about 1960 and was replaced by a German china ox in the 1990s. Baby Jesus was also broken at some point and the new resin baby came from Munich's Christmas market about ten years ago. I have seen the plaster figure designs dating back to the 1920s and 1930s, and our church (Sacred Heart, Wimbledon) used to have very similar ones in a larger size. The plaster figures are of course prone to damage and easily broken by your children, which is why plastic took over in so many firms. The styles remain the same and there are many cribs in Italy, Britain and elsewhere where the early figures are plaster and the later ones plastic, but it is impossible to tell the difference without picking them up.

*Fig 102: Italian crib by Fontanini, 6.5 cm figures with
a music box attached, c.2000*

Today, Fontanini, one of the leading Italian crib makers, based at Bagni di Lucca in North Italy since 1908, makes all its small figures from a PVC plastic which is then painted. These figures are very durable, as well as attractive, and come in various sizes and styles. The smallest are just 4.4 cm, the largest are life-size. The larger pieces are cast using a marble-based resin. The cribs are generally of a rustic stable type using real wood, bark and dried mosses. Music boxes can be fitted to them, which takes us back in time to when cribs were displayed with a musical accompaniment. The pope has a Fontanini crib in his private apartments and, in the USA,

Fig 103: Fontanini Angel, 18 cm, showing hand-painted details, 2021

there is a Fontanini Collectors Club with over 5000 members.

In Naples, the cribs still tend to be pale imitations of the 18th-century style (i.e. with clothed mannequins) but these days they are spiced up with an excess of 'personalities'. Silvio Berlusconi and other politicians are popular, as well as footballers like the late Diego Maradona, who used to play for Napoli. There are still quality traditional figures to be had, especially from makers in the Via San Gregorio Armeno, sometimes called the manger capital of the world. The proper religious crib still holds a special place in Neapolitan hearts. Look out for a small devil figure to place beneath the manger. In 2003, there was an animated film called *Opopomoz*, which featured a Neapolitan boy, jealous of the Christmas Day arrival of a new baby sister. Three devils tempt him by telling him that the birth will not happen if they transport him back in time to Bethlehem so he can prevent Jesus' birth. They can do this by using the household crib. Needless to say, the boy repents before he can do any real damage, and the devils are foiled just as they were in the medieval mystery plays.

As in Germany, many Italian shops will have cribs on display, but they will also be found in many town squares, railway stations and other public areas. A larger than life-size crib is put on display every Christmas in St Peter's Square in the Vatican.

Santons of Provence, France and Catalonia

The growth of the Provençal crib in popularity continues unabated. In 1886, the santon fair at Marseille recorded the sale of 180,000 santons, and the market has grown ever since. Christmas markets throughout France sell santon figures to the almost total exclusion of all other types of crib figures. The larger figures are still dressed with material clothes, and these can be as detailed as Neapolitan figures of an earlier age, even to the extent of detailed undergarments which are not visible. However, the more popular santon is the small painted figure just a few centimetres high. With these, huge scenes can be created covering every occupation in the village; the priest, the mayor, the school mistress, the miller, the farmer, etc. Antoine Maurel (1815–1897) wrote a Provençal Nativity story which included many characters now represented by santons. There is Roustido who arrives late because he is hard of hearing, Pimpara the knife-grinder, the simple minded Pistachie and the angel Buffarel whose cheeks are puffed up as he blows his trumpet.

Fig 104: Santon by Pierre Pagano, Marseille, c.1900

Two major early 20th-century santonierres (as santon makers are known) were Pierre and Marie-Louise Pagano from Marseille, who started painting santons before 1900. Their trade was continued by their daughter, Louise, and some wonderful examples of their work are now in the Musée des Civilisations de l'Europe et de la Mediterranée (MUCEM) in Marseille. Later, we have the Gastine sisters, Lyda (1882–1975) and Marguerite (1893–1966) who worked in Aubagne, which remains the main centre for santonierres today. They specialised in clothed santons and there was a large exhibition of their work with an accompanying publication (*L'Art at la Fantasie: Lyda et Marguerite Gastine*) in 1997.

Thérese Neveu (1866–1946) from Aubagne is often considered to be the founder of modern santons. She was the sister of the sculptor and artist Louis Sicard (1871–1946) from who she learnt her skills. She was the first santonierre to fire her santons in a kiln rather than just leaving them to air dry and she also created a huge range of new figures rather than just relying on those of the 19th century. Her figures are still copied today and the firm of Sicard is a leading santon firm in Aubagne.

Fig 105: Three santons by Thérèse Neveu from Aubagne, 11 cm high, c.1910

Santonniers today include Daniel Scaturro, who has taken a leaf out of Naples' book and makes santons of French politicians, and Daniel Coulomb, who created a bit of a stir with his santon of a pregnant Virgin Mary. The subsequent publicity led to over 1000 being sold in the first two days. Obviously, the pregnant Mary has to be replaced with a 'normal' Mary when Baby Jesus appears in the crib on Christmas Eve.

Fig 106: Santon crib figures arranged in a papier mâché cave crib,
1970s and 1980s

Santon-type figures are also produced in Catalonia, Spain, where the Caganer figure was invented for the crib. This is a peasant defecating, allegedly to fertilise the fields, but really just an excuse to put something rude into a sacred scene.

Fig 107: Caganer bought in Barcelona at the Fira de Santa Lucia in 2012

This has become such a popular figure that there are stalls at Barcelona Christmas market which sell nothing but caganers, which have now become little statues in their own right and are not only bought to be placed in a crib. Caganer politicians are unsurprisingly common, but I have seen a caganer pope, and even a caganer Darth Vader!

Matthew Powell O.P., in his *The Christmas Creche* tells us that in Provence it is the custom to say a prayer after the crib is set up which mentions all the figures there, asking God to make us 'philosophical as the fishermen, carefree as the drummer, merry as the troubadour, patient as the spinner, kind as the ass, etc'. Cynical parents might see this as a ruse to stop children asking for yet another santon for the crib since every extra figure would make the prayer longer. There must be a very long prayer after the setting up of the crib at Grignan in Provence which has 1000 figures.

*Fig 108: A set of modern hard glazed santons for use as 'beans'
in a Twelfth Night cake, 2020*

Santons can also be made small and hard glazed like those in Fig 108 in order to put them into the Twelfth Night cake, or Galette de Rois. Made like this, they are known as 'feves', or 'beans', because they replace a bean which used to be inserted into the cake. Whoever found the bean in his portion would be king for the day or master of the games to be played. Today, 'bean' santons come in many different forms; footballers, cartoon characters etc, but they were Nativity figures first of all. In France, unlike in Germany, Italy, Spain and elsewhere, you will never find large Nativities set up in shopping centres, public squares or markets because of the rigid French separation of church and state.

Spain and Portugal

The main type of Spanish and Portuguese crib tended to be small terracotta figures, rather like the santons of France and Catalonia. A centre of manufacture was Estremoz in Portugal which managed to keep the art going despite the trials of the First Republic (1910–1926) when the Catholic religion was attacked and suppressed. Mariano da Conceicao (1902–1959), the master potter at the Estremoz school of Arts and Crafts and José Sá Maria Lemos (1924–1975), the school's director, interviewed old crib makers after World War II and began producing terracotta figures again. There is an excellent example in the Glencairn Museum in Pennsylvania. Spain too had a troubled history in the 20th century with the Spanish Civil War, and crib making only revived after the Second World War, usually with the retable style of crib.

Fig 109: Retable style of Spanish crib, painted plaster, late 20th century

The retable style of crib remains very popular and can be made of terracotta or, more cheaply, in painted plaster. This style with non-moveable figures is also popular in South and Central America.

Poland

In Poland the szopka crib of Krakow retains its pre-eminence, made of wood and cardboard with an abundance of tinfoil and shiny beads. Some

Fig 110: Szopka in the procession in 2022

Fig 111: Szopka designed by
Bronislaw Piecik in 1998, Krakow

of these Nativities are so large it is difficult to spot where the Holy Family is. Since 1937 there has been a Nativity procession to the main market square in Krakow in early December, led by people dressed as shepherds and angels or in traditional Polish dress. Following them come both professional and amateur builders, as well as school entries, bearing their szopkas, which are placed around the Adam Mickiewicz monument. The best of these are awarded prizes and put on display in Krakow Museum until 23rd February.

Elsewhere in Poland, cribs of other types can be found, sometimes with figures clothed in national costume. Wood carving also remains popular, generally of a more rustic style compared to Germany.

Fig 112: Polish wooden crib with figures cast in beeswax, 2010

The crib in Fig 112 was purchased from a Polish market stall in Kingston upon Thames, selling honey and beeswax candles. The stable is made of wood, but the figures are of beeswax, The variety of materials used today to make crib figures is never ending.

Hong Kong and China

From the 1950s many cribs and crib figures were produced cheaply in plastic, firstly in the USA and then in Hong Kong. Large numbers of small self-contained plastic cribs were produced in the 1960s and 1970s in Hong Kong for the export market. The crib on the right of Fig 113

Fig 113: Plastic cribs made in Hong Kong, 1960s and 1970s, smallest is 5.2 cm high, largest 8.5 cm

was given to the author by his mother when he was a small boy in about 1970. Some cribs were made as simple Christmas ornaments for children, rather than toys. In the 1990s, China began to open up to worldwide trade and has been the centre of plastic toy production ever since.

Fig 114: Chinese made plastic crib figures in a wood and straw crib, 1994

China produces many plastic crib figures of different styles and sizes. Some, like those in Fig 114, are reasonable copies of Italian figures and can look good from a distance, others are more like comic characters aimed at the children's market. In recent years, the use of PVC and various resins has come into favour rather than hard plastic. As mentioned before, China is also the source of many copies of German Erzgebirge-style cribs in wood, and it has also recently started producing copies of Palestinian olive wood cribs.

One firm based in Hong Kong which produces some amazing quality crib figures is King & Country, a toy soldier firm, founded in 1983 by Andy Neilson and Laura Johnson. Their 1:30 scale crib figures have been thoroughly researched and are authentically dressed in Biblical costume. An interesting move was to return to the image of Our Lady lying down on her bed after the effort of giving birth. King & Country also produce figures of various later scenes from the life of Christ, although they have not yet covered the Crucifixion or Resurrection. The figures are made of lead, hand-painted, and exported around the world.

Fig 115: King & Country crib made in Hong Kong, early 21ˢᵗ century

Palestine

Pilgrims and other tourists continue to travel to the Holy Land to see the original places connected to the life of Christ, and there has always been a small tourist industry to supply souvenirs. A hundred years ago, one of the main types of souvenirs were small carvings, rosary beads and crosses made of mother of pearl from the Red Sea. Today mother of pearl is imported from Malaysia but still carved by skilled craftsmen and one of the items which can be bought is a small crib scene set into a shell.

Fig 116: Small cribs made of olive wood from Palestine, c.2000

Since the creation of Israel in 1948, if not before, local Palestinians have also carved small cribs out of olive wood left over from pruning trees. In 1989, the Catholic Near East Welfare Association helped the carvers set up a collective so that they were more adequately remunerated for their work. Now olive wood cribs, rosaries and statues are sold in large numbers to locals and tourists, and there is also a thriving export market. Small table top cribs are the most popular, but now larger pieces of olive wood are used to carve large figures up to 50 cm high, with suitably large olive wood cribs in which to stand them.

Armenia

Fig 117: Khatchar showing the Nativity with the ox and ass and the Three Kings, Sevanavank Monastery, Armenia, 13ᵗʰ century

The Armenian Church is a separate entity from other Christian churches, after it severed ties with Rome in 554. Its main form of religious imagery is a stone foliate cross carved onto an oblong stone. These are known as khatchars, and can mark graves or stand as monuments to events. They are still carved today, and small stone or wooden versions can be placed in the home. They rarely have figurative carving on them but this is not forbidden as it is the Eastern Orthodox Church. There is a khatchar at Sevanavank Monastery, dating from the 13ᵗʰ century, which has a sweet rendition of the Nativity on it in three small scenes. The top scene has Mary holding Baby Jesus, the scene below shows the ox and the ass who look as if they are sitting down to dinner (!), and the bottom scene shows the Three Wise Men.

Today, the Armenian Church has also accepted the crib, and woodcarvers are happy to make small wooden Nativities with fixed figures to display in the home. The similarity to the stone carving is clear and the vast majority of Armenian cribs are in this flat wooden style, although

Fig 118: Modern carved wooden crib from Armenia, 2018

I have seen more three-dimensional moveable figures made from clay, probably influenced from abroad.

United States of America

I have already mentioned the club of Fontanini collectors in America, and Italian and German cribs are particularly popular in the USA. The Da Prato company, founded by Italian immigrants in Massachusetts in 1860, imported plaster figures from Italy before it started manufacturing its own. Another popular form in America is the outdoor crib, usually made of highly coloured illuminated blown plastic, but flat metal silhouette cribs are also common and are spreading to other countries. Apart from Native American style cribs, which are relatively recent, the most important American crib tradition is the Moravian crib.

The Moravians are a Protestant sect which came to America in 1741 and founded the town of Bethlehem in Pennsylvania. They brought with them the custom of the German crib which they called a 'putz' (from the German 'putzen', which means 'to decorate'). Each of the three Moravian churches in Bethlehem had its crib and the idea gradually spread to people's houses, where a star is hung on the front door if the

Fig 119: Outdoor crib made of painted iron, probably American

crib is available for public viewing. Visiting other cribs was, and is, known as 'putzing'.

The figures in a Moravian crib are generally carved wooden figures in a traditional style. What makes Moravian cribs different and special is their setting. They have large layouts with the many different scenes in separate areas, such as the angel appearing to the shepherds, the visit to the inn etc. The landscape is composed of rocks moss and bark collected over the year and carefully watered to keep it fresh. The scenes can be lit up by electric light, one at a time, while a background narration tells the Christmas story. Many cribs also have water features with waterfalls and streams, which were introduced as early as the 1880s by Emmanuel Venter. A narration accompanies the crib scenes which was originally live, but is now often pre-recorded, so the effect is rather like a son et lumière production.

In 1937, the Bethlehem Chamber of Commerce declared Bethlehem to be Christmas City, USA and asked the church to create a grand putz in the Hotel Bethlehem. Two hundred people took it in turns to read the narration and operate the lights, and 40,000 visitors went along to it.

Fig 120: Lead crib figures by an unknown firm, similar to Britains or Herald, 1960s?

After the Second World War, the grand putz was moved to the Christian Education Building, where it is housed today. The landscape is rebuilt with fresh moss every year, and the crib takes about a week to construct each November. Since 1978, the Moravians have also enacted a live action Nativity pageant, with Mary on her donkey and the kings on real camels.

Great Britain

Few firms in Britain have made crib figures but, like King & Country, firms which made model soldiers did make the occasional foray into crib figure manufacturing in painted lead. As stated earlier, imported Italian cribs were those commonly seen in Britain, with the lead soldier and Hong Kong toy types coming in in the post-war period. More recently, with the growth in travel, people have visited European Christmas markets and brought home many of the crib types already discussed, but there has also always been a strong crafting tradition in this country, and many people have put their skills to making cribs and crib figures.

The author's mother was given a partial set of crib figures made principally of felt by the Catholic mystic, Caryll Houselander (1901–1954). They probably date from World War II, when Caryll helped to treat shellshocked soldiers. Mary and Baby Jesus were already missing from the set, hence its disposal and, sadly, my mother misplaced the

Fig 121: Surviving crib figures from a set by Caryll Houselander, 1940s

Three Kings later in life. The surviving figures are beautifully made with skilful needlework for the faces and wool hair. The angels are dressed in lace and have cardboard wings.

Fig 122: Paper, cardboard and cloth crib from a pattern in
Woman's Weekly Magazine, *1970s*

Fig 122. shows another homemade crib, crafted by the author and his mother when he was a teenager. The crib is manufactured from cardboard, hessian and balsa wood, whilst the figures are created from paper balls on inverted cardboard cones. The later 20th century has seen an upsurge in crafting, both because of the increase in leisure time available, and due to a widespread striving to have something individual, new and different.

Fig 123: Knitted crib by Odile Bulline from patterns by
Jean Greenhowe and Zoe Halstead

Many different patterns now exist for knitted cribs, and the internet is awash with ideas for cribs made from wooden pegs, cardboard, felt etc. Georgette Vale from Norfolk, who gives talks on her crib collection, has a mixed collection of both bought and homemade cribs which includes examples made of cardboard, clay and needle felt. She even learnt how to make stained glass so as to make a stained glass Nativity.

British churches, both Catholic and Anglican, are generally more conservative when it comes to cribs. The Catholic Our Lady of Lourdes grotto at Carfin near Motherwell in Scotland, has a crib scene erected in the 1920s with Italian figures. The whole crib was renovated in 2015, with new figures also imported from Italy. Similarly, my own church, Sacred Heart, Wimbledon, recently bought a new set of traditional

Italian figures for their crib. Previously to that, they did have a life-size Nativity with cardboard kings dressed in exotic clothes by some of the parish members, but they were not really robust enough to survive the erection and dismantling each year. Other churches sometimes try to do something different. Durham Cathedral has a wooden crib carved in the 1970s by Michael Doyle of Houghton-le-Spring, an ex-pitman who has made a crib featuring the local mining connection. The innkeeper is a miner holding a lamp, with a whippet at his side, and the ass is a pit pony.

In the 20th century the crib has also spread to all the various nonconformist churches in the UK. Whilst most of these churches are not happy with statues, they will generally have a crib on display at Christmas, and individual church members may have them in their houses. These would be used for children's education or Christmas decoration purposes and not usually as an aid to veneration in itself, as is the case within the Catholic and high Anglican churches.

Other Countries and 'Live' Cribs

Many countries round the world now produce their own style of crib reflecting their own ideas about the Nativity. The Celtic crib in Fig 124 is influenced by Celtic stone carving and is made of reconstituted stone. It has a simple design reminiscent of Armenian cribs. The Jordanian crib in Fig 124 is mostly material, with the figures made of a type of plastic or resin. Here, the holy family is housed in a Bedouin tent in the desert.

Fig 124: Celtic Irish crib produced by Past Times in the 1990s

Fig 125: Tent crib from Madaba in Jordan, 2015

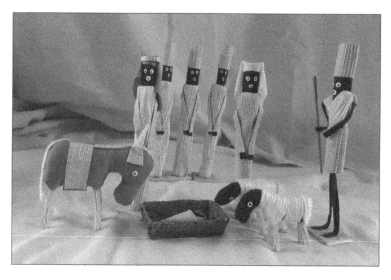

Fig 126: Modern African Crib from Tanzania or Kenya

Fig 126 shows an African crib made of material and paper which has been seen for sale to tourists in both Kenya and Tanzania. Though Jesus was born in the Middle East, He came to save us all, and so many countries like to create the scene of his birth as if it had happened in their own land, or even in a modern setting. The Crib Museum at Oberstadion, near Ulm in Germany, has its own splendid crib selection, but also puts on a different display every year. In 2020 they featured Asian cribs, including a crib set in a yurt from the central Asian steppe, and a crib from Japan made of origami. There is now so great a variety of cribs around the world that I cannot hope to cover them all here. Instead, I refer readers to James L Govan's book *The Art of the Crèche*, which covers (mostly modern) nativities from around the world (see bibliography).

Another fairly recent phenomenon is the 'live action' crib. This is different from a Nativity play in that it features a stable with real animals and actors playing the parts of Mary and Joseph, but there is no script. The actors might potter about making bread or doing carpentry and talking to each other and perhaps to the audience too. It is to give an impression of what life was like at the time of Jesus' birth, and to give children an opportunity to pet real sheep and goats etc. Cologne's medieval Christmas market has a live action crib, as do Matera and Falcone in Italy. There will be many others. Some produce it as part of a complete Medieval or Palestinian style village, where all sorts of food and crafts are for sale. In the Winter Wonderland at Hyde Park at Christmas, there is a photo booth where you can dress yourselves up as Mary and Joseph and take a picture. Not sure if that counts as a crib!

Secular and Controversial Cribs

Cribs are now well known around the world. Many firms whose majority output lies elsewhere will occasionally produce a crib. Lladro of Spain, Swarovski of Austria, Waterford of Ireland and Royal Doulton of Britain specialise in ornaments, glass and crockery, but have all made crib figures too. Even the Italian firm, Alessi, who make kitchen utensils, made a crib as a Christmas surprise one year.

Fig 127: Snowman crib made by Georgette Vale

Fig 128: Teddy Bear crib made by Georgette Vale

Since the crib scene has become so recognisable, it is possible to use different figures or even abstract shapes, and still achieve a recognisable 'crib'. Mark Oestreicher (see bibliography) has compiled a wonderful group of peculiar cribs on his web pages. One of the most popular of these non-traditional cribs is the anthropomorphic crib, especially popular with crafters. As well as the snowmen and teddy bear figures illustrated, cribs have been created with dogs, cats, sheep and even frogs and fish. In 2020, Carrie Simpson of Chester-Le-Street, County Durham, arranged a photoshoot with a dozen real dogs dressed in blankets and paper crowns to create a live action dog crib. Of course, Baby Jesus was not a dog or a teddy bear, so these cribs are perhaps less likely to be used as prayerful inspiration and aids of devotion. They are more likely to be seen as decorations and a bit of fun for most people, although it is possible some people might find them distasteful. A strange crib I particularly like is featured on the YouTube Channel of Sara Monster. It is an old plaster Italian Nativity set which has been repainted as gothic skeletons. A crib and a memento mori at the same time!

In recent years several controversial cribs have been produced. In 2004, Madame Tussauds waxworks put some of their more famous figures together in a crib scene, suitably dressed. David and Victoria Beckham stood in for Mary and Joseph. The Three Wise Men were then Prime Minister Tony Blair, President George Bush and the Duke of Edinburgh. There were also three shepherds represented by the waxworks of Samuel

L Jackson, Hugh Grant and Graham Norton. The angel was Kylie Minogue. This caused a certain amount of uproar amongst clergymen, mainly concerned about the private lives of some of these individuals. However, as one Bruce Rhodes of Winchcombe pointed out in a letter to *The Times*, many Nativity plays were put on around the country with well-known locals playing the parts whose private lives were not first investigated, and the 2004 ensemble may have at least reminded people of what Christmas was about. Nevertheless, I don't think Madame Tussauds felt it politic to repeat the experiment.

Fig 129: The Hipster Nativity of 2016 by the Modern Nativity Company

In 2016 we had the 'Hipster' crib produced by the Modern Crib Company, who tried to imagine what a Nativity scene would be like today, when the news would be spread electronically. Thus we have the man with the iPad sending the news on social media. The three Segway riders arrive with Amazon parcels. This scene is in some ways the antithesis of the crib because it is not about Jesus, who lies ignored in the manger. Instead, it shows Mary and Joseph taking a selfie. It seems more about materialism and self-centredness than humility and salvation, which is why it was criticised by some Christian groups when it came out. Cribs showing Jesus being born in a slum or refugee camp are probably less controversial; the Jesus of the Bible was born in humble circumstances, and I have seen some excellent cribs showing exactly this situation.

In 2017 there was another controversy when Greggs, the bakers, brought out an advent calendar showing various Christmas scenes and decorations interspersed with their products. The picture for Christmas Eve showed the Three Wise Men gathered in worship around the manger but, instead of Baby Jesus in the manger, there was a Greggs sausage roll. I don't think Greggs, as implied by some, was being deliberately malicious towards Christianity but they clearly didn't think the idea through. It was probably meant as a joke.

It is not just the secular world that can create controversial cribs, however. Twice in recent times, the larger than life-size crib in St Peter's Square in the Vatican has caused problems. In 2017, apart from the usual figures, the crib featured scenes of charity – the feeding of the hungry, visiting the sick and clothing the naked. This latter scene had a rather muscular naked man which was described as homoerotic by some and seen as being placed there by the gay lobby in the Vatican. The same crib was attacked by a topless female FEMEN protestor who tried to remove the Baby Jesus. The FEMEN group protests against the 'patriarchy' and had managed to snatch Baby Jesus from the Vatican crib in 2014, although he was soon retrieved and the woman arrested. The theft of the Baby Jesus is a common occurrence with outdoor accessible cribs. In this case it was to make a political statement but usually it is an attempt at obtaining a ransom, or just a simple prank. Most such cribs now have alarms or guards. The second controversial Vatican crib was in the Covid Christmas of 2020, with the lockdown preventing the creation of a new crib. The Vatican put on display a crib from the early 1970s made by students, which featured a visiting astronaut. Apart from that, the figures were also rather Dalek-like and drew scorn from much of the Catholic press.

Let us end with another controversial crib which makes a political statement. This is the Nativity by Banksy unveiled at his Walled Off Hotel in Bethlehem. While it uses traditional crib figures, the background setting is the separation wall built by Israel between that country and the Palestinian occupied territories of the West Bank. The wall has a blast hole in it shaped like a star and the piece is called *The Scar of Bethlehem*. The seemingly never-ending problems in the place where Jesus was born remind us of the troubles that faced St Jerome in this place, and the problems over the centuries faced by pilgrims trying to visit, which in turn was one of the factors encouraging the development of the Christmas crib. We are fortunate that today, with a bit of effort, pilgrims can visit Bethlehem, but all of us can still have a little Bethlehem in our own house with the Christmas crib.

Fig 130: The Scar of Bethlehem *by Banksy at the Walled Off Hotel, Bethlehem, 2019*

Conclusion

The original birthplace of Jesus became a place of devotion and a focus for prayer. The original crib was long gone by the early 4th century, and the prayer could be focussed on a silver cradle placed there by Constantine the Great. In the 13th century, supposed relics from the crib, consisting of some pieces of wood, were brought to Rome, and the Presepio Chapel in St Maria Maggiore became another centre for crib devotion. St Francis of Assisi then inspired the living crib, closely followed by the use of crib figures to recreate the scene of the Nativity. From the 13th century, the use of the crib scene as an aid to prayer was promoted by the Franciscans and later the Jesuits, and this tradition still flourishes today in both churches and private homes. From as early as the 16th century however, we see that the crib could also be a plaything for children, albeit hopefully an educational one. From the 16th century onwards, cribs were produced as works of art in their own right and the crib as a work of art flourishes to this day. The crib as a toy has developed considerably in the 20th century. Finally, we have seen that the crib has become so well known that references to it are easily recognised throughout the world, and some 'cribs' have appeared which have little connection to religious faith.

To bring people back to 'the meaning and importance of the Nativity scene', Pope Francis wrote an apostolic letter from Greccio, *Admirabile Signum*, in 2019. In it he reminds his flock that the setting up of a crib in Christian homes at Christmas time, helps us to relive the history of what took place in Bethlehem. The Gospels remain the most important source, but the portrayal of the scene helps us to imagine it, helps us to be there. As St Luke says (2:15) 'Let us go over to Bethlehem and see this thing that has happened, which the Lord has made known to us."

Bibliography

Attwater, Donald *The Penguin Dictionary of Saints*. Penguin Books London, 2nd edition 1983

Benedictine Monks of St Augustine's Abbey, Ramsgate *The Book of Saints: A Dictionary of Servants of God Canonised by the Catholic Church*. Cassell, London, 6th edition 1989

Berliner, Rudolf *Denkmäler der Krippenkunst*. Dr Filser, Augsburg 1926–30

Carter, Simon *Christmas Past Christmas Present: Four Hundred Years of English Seasonal Customs 1600-2000*. Geffrye Museum Trust Ltd 1997

Catholic Truth Society *The Crib and other Christmas Traditions*. CTS Essentials Leaflet LF40, 2006

De Robeck, Nesta *The Christmas Crib*. Burns, Oates & Washbourne Ltd, London 1938

Duffy, Eamon *The Stripping of the Altars: Traditional Religion in England c.1400-c.1580*. Yale University Press, New Haven & London, 2nd edition 2005

Ehrman, Bart D *Lost Scriptures: Books that did not make it into the New Testament*. Oxford University Press 2003

Francis, Pope *Admirabile Signum: The Meaning and Importance of the Nativity Scene*. Catholic Truth Society 2019

Gockerell, Nina *Krippen: Nativity Scenes: Creches.* Bayerisches Nationalmuseum München, Taschen 1998

Govan, James L *Art of the Crèche: Nativities from around the World.* Merrell, London & New York 2007

Grillo, Umberto *Il Presepe Napoletano: dalla Origini a San Gregorio Armeno.* Pateoli Libri 2000

Happé, Peter (ed.) *English Mystery Plays: A Selection.* Penguin Books Ltd, Harmondsworth 1975

Kempe, A J (ed.) *The Loseley Manuscripts and Other Rare Documents.* 1836 (cited by Simon Carter, see above)

Kempe, Margery *The Book of Margery Kempe.* Penguin Books 2004

Maxwell-Stuart, P G *Chronicle of the Popes: The Reign-by-reign Record of the Papacy from St Peter to the Present.* Thames & Hudson, London 1997

National Gallery, London *The First Christmas.* Francis Lincoln in association with National Gallery Publications, London, new edition 2009

Powell, Matthew, O.P. *The Christmas Crèche : Treasure of Faith, Art & Theater.* Pauline Books & Media, Boston 1997

Ringler, Josef *Deutsche Weihnachtskrippen: Eine Auslese deutscher Krippenkunst aus vier Jahrhunderten.* Verlagsanstalt Tyrolia, Innsbruck, Vienna, Munich 1929

Sweitzer, Vangie Roby *Christmas in Bethlehem: A Moravian Heritage.* Central Moravian Church, Bethlehem, Pennsylvania 2000

Tixier, Jean-Max *La Crèche et les Santons de Provence.* Aubanel 2000

Von Boehn, Max *An Illustrated History of Table Decorations and the Christmas Crib.* Read Books 2011 Reprint of 1920s? original

Websites

https://en.wikipedia.org/wiki/Nativity_scene Wikipedia history of the Neapolitan crib

https://en.wikipedia.org/wiki/Sacro_Monte_di_Varallo
Website concerning this 'Sacred Mountain'

https://www.bayerisches-nationalmuseum.de/index.php?id=287&L=1 Webpages concerning the Max Schmederer Crib Collection in the Bavarian National Museum, Munich

https://bloghistoriadelarte.wordpress.com/2013/12/10/el-arte-de-los-belenes-the-art-of-Nativity-scene/ *Comprehensive blogpost on crib history*

www.krippenmuseum.com Website of the Maranatha Nativity Museum in Luttach-Ahrntal, Italy

www.metmuseum.org/art/collection/search Search this site of the Metropolitan Museum of Art in New York for the Neapolitan crib figures donated by Loretta Lines Howard in 1964

http://www.tradicioun.org/La-creche-Provencale Superb website on the history of the Provencal crib and the santons

www.unfoeprae.org Website of the Universalis Foederatio Praesepistica (World Federation of Friends of Cribs)

The 77 Weirdest Nativities (2017 edition)! | whyismarko (Mark Oestreicher of the Youth Cartel has created a list of the strangest nativities you will ever come across!)

Names for the Christmas Crib

The Crib goes by various names in different countries and I thought it useful to list the more common ones here.

Belen	Spain and Provence
Betlem	Czech Republic
Creche	France and USA
Crib	UK and Ireland
Krippe	Germany and Austria
Nativity Scene	Generic English
Pesebre	Spain
Presepe	Italy
Presepio (Latin)	Italy and Portugal
Putz	Moravian Church, USA
Szopka	Poland

APPENDIX 2

The Figures in the Crib

A list of the more usual figures in the crib and their characteristics.

Main Figures

Baby Jesus   The heart of any crib scene, usually depicted lying in the manger on a heap of straw with a small loin cloth, but sometimes in Mary's arms.

Mary   The mother of Jesus. Also known as the Virgin Mary or Our Lady. Generally depicted kneeling and wearing red and blue. Copied from medieval artists, these colours were used for the most important people in paintings.

Joseph   St Joseph may be kneeling or standing. He often carries a candle or lamp and is frequently depicted wearing brown and purple, although the origin of those colours is uncertain. In Neapolitan cribs, a yellow cloak is usual.

     The above three figures are often called The Holy Family or, in Italy, 'The Mystery'.

Ox and Ass   May be standing or lying, sometimes breathing on Jesus to keep him warm. The Ass often carries Mary to Bethlehem, and later carries Mary on the Flight into Egypt.

Shepherds   May wear classical or contemporary costumes. One may carry a lamb as a gift. Another is often depicted

	with bagpipes or another musical instrument. Often accompanied by more sheep.
Three Kings	Usually kings these days rather than Magi (Wise Men). Sometimes depicted as coming from Europe, Asia and Africa. More often now shown as one old, one young and one black. In Germany the black king is normally Melchior, in Spain Balthasar, and I have seen a 17th century Dutch painting (Jan van Bijlert) of a black king where he is called Caspar. Likewise, I have seen the old King called both Caspar and Balthasar. The names first appear in the early 6th century. They may kneel or stand and may be accompanied by servants, horses, camels and elephants in more elaborate cribs. They have their treasures of gold, frankincense and myrrh.
Angels	Any number of angels can be in the crib or above it, with the star. Gabriel is the angel of the Annunciation. Michael sometimes leads the choir of angels in Heaven
The Star	Most cribs now have a star attached or displayed in some way.

Occasional Figures (See also Chapter Five for figures particular to Neapolitan and Provençal cribs)

God the Father	God the Father is sometimes depicted with the angels in Heaven
Prophets	Some cribs may have Elijah and Isaiah as the prophets who foretold the birth of Jesus.
Sybil	Some cribs may have a Sybil as a foreteller, sometimes speaking to Emperor Augustus.
Cockerel	Portuguese cribs often have a cockerel crowing the good news.
'The Wonder'	A woman who stands in awe and amazement before Baby Jesus. A figure found in cribs of Bologna.
'The Sleeper'	A sleeping man in the background of the crib. The opposite of 'The Wonder' this is the man who sleeps

through this most important event. Another figure from cribs of Bologna.

Caganer	Catalan and Provencal cribs often have a caganer as a figure of fun in the crib. One might translate it as Defecator.
Lou Ravi	Another popular Provencal figure who stands amazed with a blissful expression and his arms raised in wonder. A lucky figure often placed first in the crib. Sometimes called the village idiot, which is a little unfair.
Napoleon	Many French cribs have a figure of Napoleon from a time when crib figure manufacture was frowned upon. Napoleon figures showed loyalty to the government.
Pope	Many French cribs also have a figure of the pope in thanks for the concordat signed between Napoleon and Pope Pius VII in 1801.
Midwives	The two midwives who helped with the birth are now rarely depicted.
Devil	Some Neapolitan cribs have a devil below the manger in a memory of the medieval Nativity plays.
Simeon & Anna	These two figures, Simeon the High Priest and Anna the Prophetess, were present at the Presentation in the Temple and feature in scenes dedicated to that event, but may also appear in an ordinary crib as onlookers.

Since Jesus was born for all of us, there is of course room in the crib for everyone, and every class, trade, nationality, etc, has been depicted in a crib at some point.

APPENDIX 3

Crib Museums

Sadly, there are no dedicated crib museums or galleries in Great Britain, but there are occasional displays. Most museums in Germany and Italy will have at least one old crib on show, especially during advent.

The Victoria and Albert Museum has at least two cribs though these are not usually on display. It also has some Nativity scene sculptures by Della Robbia and Pisano, and it has a 16th century rocking cradle.

The National Gallery, London, has an excellent collection of Nativity art.

The Bavarian National Museum in Munich has perhaps the best collection of German and Neapolitan cribs.

The Crib Museum in Oberstadion has some excellent traditional and modern cribs, and changing exhibitions.

The Maranatha Nativity Museum in Luttach, South Tyrol, has changing displays of contemporary woodcarving, including cribs.

The Käthe Wohlfahrt shop in Rothenberg on the Tauber has a Christmas Museum which has a variety of German cribs from the last 150 years.

The Musée des Civilisations de l'Europe et de la Mediterranée (MUCEM) in Marseille has a wonderful collection of Provençal santons.

The Stadtmuseum of Steyr, near Linz, in Austria has an excellent collection of early paper and card cribs.

Best of all, go to any Christmas Market in Western Europe (except Britain!) and you will see a great variety of contemporary cribs and crib figures. Many towns will also have old and new cribs on show during advent.

Index

155

Christmas Crib History Figure List

Fig 1   The Church of the Nativity at Bethlehem with the Door of Humility to the left. (Wikimedia Commons)

Fig 2   The Grotto in the Church of the Nativity. (Wikimedia Commons, photographer Darko Tepert Donatus)

Fig 3   The Grotto in the Church of the Nativity. The site of Jesus' birth. (Wikimedia Commons, photographer Darko Tepert Donatus)

Fig 4   The Reliquary of the crib in Santa Maria Maggiore in Rome. (Wikimedia Commons)

Fig 5   Roman gravestone from Naxos showing the ox and ass with Jesus. *c.*400. (Byzantine Museum, Athens)

Fig 6   Mary presents Jesus to the three Magi with their camels. One points to the star. A 4th century AD Roman sarcophagus from St Agnes, Rome. (Vatican Museum)

Fig 7   The Magi follow the star. A Byzantine Mosaic in Sant' Apollinaire Nuovo in Ravenna, dating to the early 7th Century. This is the earliest known occurrence of names for the Magi. (Wikimedia Commons, photographer Nina Aldin Thune)

Fig 8   Nativity scene from the 12th century Winchester Bible in Winchester Cathedral Library. (Winchester Cathedral postcard by Sonia Halliday)

Fig 9   Byzantine icon showing old, young and black Magi, now crowned as kings, on the middle left, and the two midwives washing Jesus at bottom right, 15th century. (Byzantine Museum, Athens)